Robert Allen Campbell

Our Flag

The Evolution of the Stars and Stripes

Robert Allen Campbell

Our Flag
The Evolution of the Stars and Stripes

ISBN/EAN: 9783742808608

Manufactured in Europe, USA, Canada, Australia, Japa

Cover: Foto ©Thomas Meinert / pixelio.de

Manufactured and distributed by brebook publishing software
(www.brebook.com)

Robert Allen Campbell

Our Flag

THE COLONIAL FLAG—DECEMBER 13, 1775.

FLAG OF THE UNITED STATES.

THE ORIGINAL STARS AND STRIPES—JUNE 14, 1777.

OUR FLAG

OR THE EVOLUTION OF

THE STARS AND STRIPES

INCLUDING THE REASON TO BE OF THE DESIGN
THE COLORS AND THEIR POSITION
MYSTIC INTERPRETATION

TOGETHER WITH

SELECTIONS ELOQUENT, PATRIOTIC AND POETICAL

BY ROBERT ALLEN CAMPBELL

CHICAGO
H. E. LAWRENCE & CO.
96 STATE STREET

TO

EVERY MAN AND WOMAN

WHO LOVES OUR FLAG

AS THE EMBLEM OF

GOVERNMENT OF THE PEOPLE, BY THE PEOPLE, FOR THE PEOPLE

WHO HAILS THE STARS AND STRIPES

AS THE

HOPE OF ALL WHO SUFFER AND THE DREAD OF ALL WHO WRONG

WHO REVERES THE RED, WHITE AND BLUE

AS THE SYMBOL OF

ASPIRATION, INTELLIGENCE AND INDUSTRY

WHICH WILL IN DUE TIME

ESTABLISH AND MAINTAIN

THE UNIVERSAL BROTHERHOOD OF MAN

THIS LITTLE BOOK IS

BY THE AUTHOR

FRATERNALLY

DEDICATED

PREFACE.

THIS outline sketch of the origin, evolution and history of the Stars and Stripes is, in the main, of course, a compilation of facts and dates from official sources, larger works, occasional pamphlets and addresses upon this and collateral subjects; and it is meant, therefore, for the perusal of those who have not the time, opportunity or disposition for a more extended study in this line of research. This plain statement renders it unnecessary to use "quotation marks" or to give special credits, for the author is responsible for only the general plan of the work and for the arrangement of the materials.

That part of this sketch which treats of the proceedings of the Congressional Committee in relation to the Colonial Flag, and of the unofficial consideration, by a few of our Revolutionary statesmen and heroes, in regard to the Flag of the "Thirteen United States," immediately preceding its adoption by Congress, has not heretofore been published. These proceedings and arguments give the real reasons for the adoption of the colors in our National Standard and for its design; and they incidentally furnish the foundation for the correspondential value, esoteric interpretation and mystic meaning—

the reason to be—of the Stars and Stripes as our
National Standard.

The Selections, Eloquent, Patriotic and Poetical,
comprise a few extracts and poems, which, though
old and oft repeated, are always new in their loveli-
ness, and "blessedly commonplace" as household
and heart-warming words—beautiful in their sentiment and expression.

EXPLANATION.

The flags illustrated in this volume are engraved
in such a way that the direction of the shading
indicates the color.

Perpendicular lines represent Red.

Horizontal lines represent Blue.

Oblique lines, running downward from left to
right, represent Green.

CONTENTS.

CHAPTER I.
Early Flags of America, - - - - - 9
CHAPTER II.
The Colonial Flag, - - - - - - 35
CHAPTER III.
The Stars and Stripes, - - - - - 55
CHAPTER IV.
Selections—Eloquent, Patriotic and Poetical, - 97

ILLUSTRATIONS.

1. American Flag, - - - - Frontispiece.
2. Isabella, - - - - - - - - 9
3. Columbus, - - - - - - - - 11
4. Landing of Columbus, - - - - 14
5. Spanish Flag, - - - - - - 15
6. Flag of the Expedition, - - - - 15
7. John Cabot, - - - - - - - 17
8. Cross of St. George, - - - - - 19
9. English Union, - - - - - - 19
10. Heinrich Hudson, - - - - - 21
11. Dutch W. I. Co. Flag, - - - - - 21
12. Bunker Hill Flag, - - - - - 27
13. Pine Tree Flag, - - - - - - 27
14. Pine Tree Union Flag, - - - - 29
15. Rattle-snake Flag, - - - - - - 29

16. South Carolina Flag, -   -   -   -   32
17. Washington, -   -   -   -   -   -   - 34
18. Franklin, -   -   -   -   -   -   - 43
19. The Colonial Flag, -   -   -   -   -   - 49
20. White Plains Flag,   -   -   -   -   52
21. John Paul Jones, -   -   -   -   -   - 52
22. John Hancock, -   -   -   -   -   - 54
23. Original Stars and Stripes,   -   -   -   - 63
24. Stars and Stripes—1818,   -   -   -   - 82
25. Naval Union—May 18, 1818, -   -   -   - 83
26. Naval Union—September 18, 1818,   -   -   84
27. Flag of Texas,   -   -   -   -   -   - 87

NOTE.— The United States Standard Flag is spoken of as containing forty-four stars in the Union. This will be true after July 4, 1891. The law upon the subject is that new stars to the Union, to represent new States, will be added on July 4th next succeeding the admission of the State. The official United States Flag, therefore, from July 4, 1890, to July 4, 1891, contains forty-three stars in the Union—Wyoming being admitted after July 4, 1890.

OUR FLAG.

CHAPTER I.

EARLY FLAGS IN AMERICA.

Every department of the early history of the American Continent must be more or less intimately

ISABELLA.

and directly connected with Isabella of Castile, Queen of Spain, without whose timely assistance the New World would not have been so soon discovered.

In 1484 Christopher Columbus appeared at the Royal Court of Spain, where he presented to the sovereigns, Ferdinand and Isabella, his theories concerning a westward route to the Indies, and submitted to them his plans for thus reaching the eastern shores of Asia, and by the right of discovery adding rich and extensive dependencies to the Spanish domain. He was courteously received, and after frequent and protracted delays his proposals were submitted to a "council of learned men," for their opinion concerning Columbus and his enterprising adventure. They listened to the navigator attentively, discussing his theories exhaustively from their scientific, religious, and pecuniary points of view. After mature deliberation, they pronounced the whole scheme as one which was "vain, impractical, and resting on grounds too weak to merit the support of the government." A small minority of this council considered the matter more favorably, among them Father Perez, a former confessor of Isabella.

The Queen was favorably impressed with Columbus, and she had great faith in Father Perez and his associates who endorsed the navigator and recommended his enterprise. She was, therefore, heartily in favor of granting Columbus all necessary aid.

King Ferdinand, who failed to grasp the grand possibilities of the result in case of success, and who had no liking for Columbus nor any confidence in his theories, and who never had any intention toward any outlay of money in the venture, gladly accepted the decision of the "learned council;" and he, therefore, refused any recognition of or any assistance to what was considered, by him and his advisers, "the chimerical conceit of a deluded enthusiast."

COLUMBUS.

He likewise opposed the Queen when she was considering the advisability of giving to Columbus her individual endorsement and assistance.

Columbus left Madrid discouraged and almost hopeless, intending to seek possible but not very probable assistance in France. Father Perez and his associates made another appeal to Isabella, appealing so successfully to her love of Spanish enterprise and her religious zeal that she dispatched a courier to overtake the would-be discoverer and bring him back.

Isabella was of medium size, well formed, with a fair complexion, auburn hair and clear blue eyes. There was a mingled gravity and dignity in her bearing, and her sweetness of countenance and singular modesty graced a great firmness of purpose and a deep earnestness of spirit. She was a beautiful combination of resolute and active qualities, usually considered masculine, purified and ennobled by the enthusiasm and kindly charity of woman. She determined that she would give to Columbus the royal recognition and furnish him the pecuniary assistance that would enable him to undertake his cherished voyage of discovery; and her celebrated final answer to her associate sovereign and husband—and to his learned counselors—who opposed her bitterly in this decision which she made "for the glory and benefit of Spain and the Church," is a clear indication and a good illustration of her character. Standing before them in resolute dignity, her eyes and gesture announcing a not-to-be-changed determination, she said, " I will assume the undertaking—for my own crown of Castile; and I am ready to pawn my jewels to defray the expense of it—if the funds in the treasury shall appear inadequate. "

Isabella furnished and fitted out two small vessels, the *Pinta* and the *Mina*. These were small coasting *Caravels*, with partial decks fore and aft, but no deck amidships; and they were provided with oars to be used in case of a calm or light wind, when their limited sails would be comparatively useless. The *Santa Maria*, which Columbus, through the influence and assistance of a wealthy and enterprising Spanish family, the Pinzons, secured and supplied, was somewhat larger and had a full deck.

It thus came about that when the enthusiastic and adventurous Columbus, with the Pinzons and about one hundred and twenty subordinates, embarked in his miniature fleet of very inferior vessels and sailed away from the European coast on his voyage of discovery across the western waste of unexplored waters, his ships carried the flag of Castile and Leon, and the special flag of the expedition.

After many days of constant watching and as many nights of monotonous anxiety, in which hope and fear alternately predominated, his eyes were gladdened and his heart was cheered by the discovery of hitherto unknown land. Columbus and a goodly number of his crews at once disembarked, and with much pomp and in all due solemnity he took possession of the New World in the name of, and as the property of, his sovereign; and he planted upon the new-found shore the Royal Standard of Spain, and with it the flag of his expedition. And these are the first flags, of which we have any reliable

or definite account, that were ever unfurled to the
air west of the Atantic.

LANDING OF COLUMBUS.

Supposed to have been drawn by himself.

This important event, which occurred at the Island of San Salvador on October 12, 1492, is graphically described by the younger Columbus, who was an eye-witness of the proceedings, as follows:

"Columbus, dressed in scarlet, first stepped on shore from the little boat which bore him from his vessels, bearing the Standard of Spain, emblazoned with the arms of Castile and Leon (a turretted and

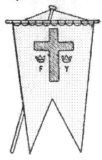

SPANISH FLAG.   EXPEDITION FLAG.

embattled castle *or*, on a field *gules*, for Castile, quarterly on a field *argent*, a lion rampant *gules*, for Leon) in his own hand, followed by the Pinzons in their own boats, each bearing the banner of the expedition, which was a white flag with a green cross, having, on each side, the letters F and Y, surmounted by golden crowns."

Six years later Columbus landed on the shore of the continent, at the mouth of the Orinoco; and, of course, he took possession of the country by announcing such fact to his followers and the neighboring trees, and by planting there the Spanish Standard.

Columbus supposed he had found an island near the mainland of Eastern Asia; and he died without knowing his error in this respect—for he never knew he had discovered a new continent.

Americus Vespucius, in 1497, discovered the main land of the Western Continent at Yucatan; and two years later he landed at several places north of the Orinoco. He, as was the custom of the times, invariably went through the formal ceremony of claiming the country visited, for his government; and took possession in the name of his sovereign by erecting thereupon the Spanish colors. In 1507 he made the first announcement that all these points which Columbus and himself had visited were not on the eastern shore of Asia, but that an entirely new, and hitherto unthought-of, continent had been discovered. It thus came that the new continent, which he first announced, was named in his honor.

It is altogether probable, that in June, 1497, John Cabot, with his sons and associates, planted the English Standard and the Venetian Banner of St. Mark upon the coast of what is now known as Labrador; and that during the following year Sebastian Cabot visited what is now the eastern coast of the New England States; and that he erected the British colors at various places where he landed.

During the summer of 1527 John Rut visited many places on the main land between the mouth of the St. Lawrence and the Carolinas. Various expeditions during the sixteenth century visited the

Western World; and each one of them went through the formality of taking possession of the localities where they landed, in the name of their government

JOHN CABOT.

and king; and at each place thus visited they raised for a time the English Flag.

The British Standard used by the Cabots and other English navigators during this time was probably the Cross of St. George, which is a white flag with a rectangular red cross extending the entire length and height of the banner. This was doubtless the first—and during the sixteenth century almost the only—flag planted in any part of the territory which is now the United States.

A French Colony settled at Arcadia—now Annapolis, in 1605; but what flag, if any, they set up does not appear in any report concerning the settlement. It is altogether probable, however, that they displayed some one of the numerous banners then in use by the French people.

When the Mayflower sailed away from England, she probably wore the cross of St. George as a secondary banner, while she carried the British National Standard at the maintop. This was the "King's Colors," or Union Flag, frequently then called the Union Jack; and it was a combination of the cross of St. George—the former English Flag—and the cross of St. Andrew, or Scotch Standard. The latter was a blue flag, with a diagonal white cross extending from corner to corner. The King's Colors was, therefore, a blue flag, with a rectangular red cross and a diagonal white cross, all meeting in the center of the field. The red cross showed entire, the arms extending to the sides and the ends of the field, while the white cross extended from corner to corner diagonally, but was interrupted at the center by the red cross.

The cross of St. George was in common use in

the American Colonies of England; and it was the occasion of considerable trouble among the Puritans, for many of them looked upon it as an emblem of Romanism, and, hence, of idolatry and Anti-Christ.

The English Parliament, in 1651, changed the National Standard from the Union Flag—the combined crosses of St. George and St. Andrew—to the former alone, as it had been before the union of

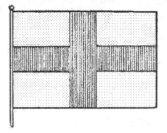

ST. GEORGE'S CROSS.   ENGLISH UNION.

the English and Scotch banners; and the General Court of Massachusetts followed suit in also adopting the same flag for the standard of the Colony.

A flag frequently seen in New England during the latter part of the Seventeenth and the early part of the Eighteenth century was the St. George's cross, its center ornamented with a yellow, or gilt, crown, under which was the King's monogram in black.

A common flag in the same locality about this time, and later on, was a field of crimson, or blue or green, with a white union, in which was a St. George's cross. A tree, or hemisphere, or other device, often occupied the upper staff corner of the union. Sometimes this device replaced the entire St. George's cross, so that the unwelcome suggestion of Romanism did not appear on the flag.

The British Parliament, in 1707, re-adopted the Union Flag as the British Standard; and this, with many modifications, was used by all the English Colonies in America from that time until the adoption of Stars and Stripes, after the Declaration of Independence.

The present English Union (a combination of the crosses of St. George, for England; St. Andrew, for Scotland; and St. Patrick—a red diagonal—for Ireland) was adopted in 1801; and it has, therefore, never been used, of course, as a government flag over any territory now belonging to the United States.

Heinrich Hudson was probably the first European who landed upon the shores of the Western World, at what is now New York. There he raised the standard of the Netherlands; and that flag he carried at his masthead as he first explored the beautiful river which has ever since borne his name. The Dutch Standard, at that time, was a flag of three equally wide, longitudinal stripes—orange above, white in the middle, and blue below. As Hudson was in the employ of the Dutch East India Company, he naturally displayed their flag—which was

HEINRICH HUDSON.

the one above described, with the addition of the letters " A. O. C." in black on the center of the white stripe. This was the official flag of the Manhattan Colony from 1609—the date of Hudson's first landing at that place — until 1622, when the Colony passed to the control of the Dutch West India Company,

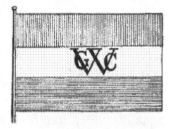

DUTCH FLAG.

and the letters on the flag were then changed to
" G. W. C."

In 1650, the Government of the Netherlands,
changed the orange stripe on their flag to one of red
and this continued the standard colors of the colony
until 1664, when Manhattan surrendered to the English.   Then the Dutch name, New Amsterdam, was
changed to New York; and the red, white and blue
of Holland gave way to the red, white and blue of
the British Union Flag.

The Dutch Flag was, however, again, for a short
time, the acknowledged standard—from July, 1673,
to November, 1674.   From this time New York was
under the British Flag until it was displaced to make
way for the triumphant Stars and Stripes.

It was, therefore, in 1650, at New Amsterdam,
that the " Red, White and Blue " was first, in stripes,
unfurled to the breeze as the colors and fundamental
design destined to become permanent, victorious and
glorious as the Flag of the Free Republic.

Roger Williams, who was born one of the common people, among the hills of Wales, and who in
his native land was an humble parish priest of the
English Church, left his European home, emigrating
to the American Colonies, hoping to find there—
what was denied him in Great Britain—freedom to
worship God in accordance with his own ideas upon
that subject.   In this expectation he was sorely dis-
appointed; for he found New England as intolerant
as Old England, and he was soon exiled from Massa-

chusetts on account of his heresies. With a few others he formed a small settlement, calling it the Providence Plantations, in what is now Rhode Island.

For this little Colony he secured a grant from the English Goverment; and on July 8, 1663, the original royal grant was confirmed by Charles II., who on that day issued the Rhode Island Charter.

This charter was, in some respects, very different from any Governmental or Royal decree ever before issued. It was the first governmental acknowledgment the world ever saw, of two fundamental principles in regard to the rights of man, as man—that is, in regard to the rights of the individual citizen as related to the sovereign, or to the people as a State or Nation.

First: The original rights of the natives of the soil were acknowledged in the other Colonies, as against the rights of the Colonial Emigrants; but these rights of the Indians were considered and treated as subordinate to the rights of the English King. That is, the royal grant preceded the actual purchase from the Indians; and this purchase from the Red Man was more in the nature of good policy than because it was considered any transfer of actual ownership. In Rhode Island, the Royal grant followed the Indian title-deed; and the former was never in that Colony accepted as sufficient of itself to justify the driving out of the Indian and the occupancy of his territory. This doctrine of the primary rights of the Indian was, in fact, one of the

heresies for which Massachusetts punished Roger
Williams by banishing him into exile.

Second. The other principle of individual human
rights, first given Governmental sanction in the Charter of Rhode Island—and which, to the Colonists then
as well as to all mankind then and thereafter, is of
far more importance than any question of property—
was the absolute right of each citizen to perfect freedom in regard to all religious matters—whether
of faith or practice. This latter right of the individual to his absolute liberty in matters of religion
and worship is stated in that charter in the following terms: "Noe person within the sayd Colonye,
at any tyme hereafter, shall be any wise molested,
punished, disquieted, or called in question, for any
difference of opinion in matters of religion which doe
not actually disturb the civill peace of our sayd
Colonye; but that all and everye person may, from
tyme to tyme, and at all tymes hereafter, freelye and
fullye have and enjoy his and their own judgments
and consciences, in matters of religious concernments,
through the tract of lands hereafter mentioned, they
behaving themselves peaceablie and quietlie, and not
using this libertye to licentiousness and profaneness,
nor to the civill injurye or outward disturbance of
others—any law, statute or clause therein contained,
or to be contained, usage or custom of this realm, to
the contrary hereof, in any wise, notwithstanding."

About twenty years later William Penn, the
Quaker, pursued a similar policy to that of Roger

Williams, the Baptist, with the Indians; and he also announced to his new settlements, in what is now Pennsylvania, a similar law of religious freedom and toleration. Whether these two grand reformers in the realms of practical religion and philanthropy consulted with or patterned after each other—or whether they each came to his own conclusions and announced his own theory and practice independ- ently—is not now known.   Certain it is, however, that the absolute right of each individual to the dis- posal of his own property, as well as to his own creed and practice in religion, independent of any princely or priestly domination, first had practical recognition in Rhode Island and Pennsylvania. In both these instances the Divine truth of individual freedom was announced and defended, illustrated and established, by men who had themselves suffered from the per- secutions of princes and priests; and who, through courage, effort and suffering, had achieved for them- selves the rights which they taught to and secured for others.

It was the recognition, announcement and gen- eral acceptance of this grand underlying principle of individual religious liberty that rendered the inde- pendence of the Colonies desired and possible; for the individual right to adopt or form a creed, and to accept or invent a ceremony to express that creed, must, sooner or later, bear the natural fruit of laws and administration satisfactory to the majority of the nation.

It took this principle of individual liberty more than a century to so develop in the minds of the Colonists that they demanded its full recognition— and hence needed a symbol to announce its comparative maturity. That symbol came—as we will see— in the form of the Stars and Strips—the Red, White and Blue. During Colonial days there were many different flags carried by companies of men who were organized permanently, or gathered together temporarily, for operations against their enemies— mainly the Indians.

In the times of the earlier and later differences between the Colonies and the Mother country there were many modifications of the English Flag, and there were many independent, local, regimental and colonial standards, to catalogue and describe which would require a ponderous volume.

There is no authentic account of what flag, if any, was displayed by the Americans at either Lexington or Bunker Hill in 1775. One writer says that the flag of the colonists at Bunker Hill was one having a blue field with a white Union, in which was a red cross, and in the upper staff corner a green pine tree. Another author describes the same flag as to design, on that memorable occasion, but makes the field red instead of blue. It is probable that both flags were there, simultaneously or successively, carried by different companies; for it is well established that such red and blue colors were in use about that time in the New England Colonies.

The Connecticut troops, in 1775, carried banners of solid color—a different color for each regiment—yellow, blue, scarlet, crimson, white, azure, blue and orange. These flags bore on one side the motto, "*Qui transtulit sustinet*," and on the other side "An Appeal to Heaven."

On October 20, 1775, General Washington asked two of his corresponents, "Please fix upon some particular flag, and a signal by which our vessels

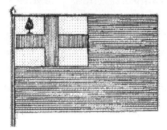

BUNKER HILL FLAG.   PINE TREE FLAG.

may know one another. What do you think of a flag with a white ground, a tree in the middle, the motto, '*An Appeal to Heaven?*'"

The cruisers fitted out by order of the Continental Congress, in the fall of 1775, were sent out with the pine tree standard.

The Massachusetts Council, in the spring of 1776, adopted for a standard, to be used in her sea service, a white flag with a green pine tree, and the inscription, "An Appeal to Heaven." Frequent mention is made of this flag—with frequent minor modifications—as being carried by military companies, war vessels, privateers, and merchantmen; and a flag of this device, worn by a military company of Newburyport, is now in the museum of Independence Hall, Philadelphia.

A modification of the Pine Tree Flag, which was also common, was one, the field of which was red or blue, with a white union, and in this union the green pine tree, with or without a motto.

The Pine Tree Banner divided its popularity with the almost as plentiful varying devices of the Rattlesnake emblem; for this was a favorite symbol, and of very frequent occurrence during Colonial and Revolutionary times.

The Colonies were, in all their contests with the Indians and their French allies, acting with only partial co-operation. In order to impress upon the people the necessity for united and co-operative action, Dr. Franklin, in 1754, published in his *Gazette* an engraving of a curved rattlesnake, which appeared divided into several parts, each of which bore a name. The head was called New England, and the other parts were each given the name of one of the other Colonies. Under this suggestive device was the motto "*Unite or Die.*" Similar symbols were published in other papers at different times later; and the rattlesnake, in various attitudes and combinations, appeared, upon drumheads, medals and flags, often accompanied with the motto, "*Don't Tread on Me.*"

The following interesting suggestions concerning the rattlesnake as an emblem are usually attributed to Benjamin Franklin; but there are grave doubts as to their real authorship. They were published in the Pennsylvania *Gazette* of December 27, 1775.

"Messrs. Printers:—I observed that on one of the drums belonging to the marines, now raising, there was painted a rattlesnake, with this modest motto under it, 'Don't tread on me!' As I know it is the

PINE TREE FLAG.   RATTLESNAKE FLAG.

custom to have some device on the arms of every country, I supposed this might be intended for the arms of North America. As I have nothing to do with public affairs, and as my time is perfectly my own, in order to divert an idle hour, I sat down to guess what might have been intended by this uncommon device. I took care, however, to consult on this occasion a person acquainted with heraldry, from whom I learned that it is a rule among the learned in that science that the worthy properties of an animal in a crest shall be considered, and that the

base ones cannot have been intended. He likewise
informed me that the ancients considered the serpent
as an emblem of wisdom; and, in certain attitudes,
of endless duration; both of which circumstances, I
suppose, may have been in view. Having gained
this intelligence, and recollecting that countries are
sometimes represented by animals peculiar to them,
it occurred to me that the rattlesnake is found only
in America; and that it may, therefore, have been
chosen on that account to represent her. But then
the worthy properties of a snake, I judged, would be
hard to point out. This rather raised than sup-
pressed my curiosity; and having frequently seen the
rattlesnake, I ran over in my mind every property
for which she was distinguished, not only from other
animals, but from those of the same genus or class,
endeavoring to fix some meaning to each not wholly
inconsistent with common sense. I recollected that
her eye exceeded in brightness that of any other
animal, and that she had no eyelids. She may
therefore be esteemed an emblem of vigilance. She
never begins an attack, nor, when once engaged,
surrenders. She is, therefore, an emblem of magna-
nimity and true courage. As if anxious to prevent
all pretensions of quarreling with the weapons with
which nature favored her, she conceals them in the
roof of her mouth, so that, to those who are unac-
quainted with her, she appears most defenseless; and
even when these weapons are shown and extended
for defense, they appear weak and contemptible;

but their wounds, however small, are decisive and fatal. Conscious of this, she never wounds until she has generously given notice—even to her enemy, and cautioned him against the danger of treading on her. Was I wrong, sirs, in thinking this a strong picture of the temper and conduct of America?

" The poison of her teeth is the necessary means of digesting her food, and, at the same time, is the certain destruction of her enemies. This may be understood to intimate that those things which are destructive to our enemies may be to us not only harmless, but absolutely necessary to our existence. I confess I was totally at a loss what to make of the rattles until I went back and counted them, and found them just *thirteen*— exactly the number of Colonies united in America; and I recollected, too, that this was the only part of the snake which increased in numbers. Perhaps it may have been only my fancy, but I conceited the painter had shown a half-formed additional rattle, which I suppose may have been intended to represent the Province of Canada. 'Tis curious and amazing to observe how distinct and independent of each other the rattles of this animal are, and yet how firmly they are united together, so as to be never separated except by breaking them in pieces. One of these rattles, singly, is incapable of producing any sound; but the ringing of the thirteen together is sufficient to alarm the boldest man living. The rattlesnake is solitary, and associates with her kind only when it is necessary

for her preservation. In winter, the warmth of a
number together will preserve their lives, whilst
singly they would probably perish. The power of
fascination attributed to her, by a generous construction, may be understood to mean that those who consider the liberty and blessings which America affords,·
and once come over to her, never afterwards leave
her, but spend their lives with her. She strongly
resembles America in this: that she is beautiful in
youth, and her beauty increases with age; her
tongue is also blue, and
forked as lightning, and
her abode is among the
impenetrable rocks."

The earliest standard
displayed in the South
which was distinctively
American, but still not at
SOUTH CAROLINA FLAG.   all National, was one designed by Colonel Moul-
trie, and by him raised at Charleston, South Carolina, in the fall of 1775. It was a large blue flag with
a white crescent in the upper corner near the staff.
Colonel Moultrie subsequently modified the design
by adding the word "LIBERTY," in large white
letters.

The first flag in America which bore the thirteen
stripes, as a part of its design, is supposed by some
authorities to have been one which Captain Abra-
ham Markoe presented to his military company, " The

Philadelphia Troop of Light Horse," organized in the fall of 1774. The flag was designed, or, at least, drawn, by John Folwell, and painted by James Claypoole, in September, 1775. This standard is still kept as a precious relic in Philadelphia, where the 'City Troop of Philadelphia" have built a fire and burglar proof vault for its preservation. This flag is a double one, forty inches long and thirty-four wide; the design is very elaborate, and its execution very rich. The thirteen stripes of blue and silver form the upper union and occupy a space twelve and one-half inches long by nine and one-half inches deep.

The probability is that the thirteen stripes were not originally upon the flag, but that they were introduced at a time subsequent to its presentation. Upon this point, however, there is room for a difference of opinion.

WASHINGTON.

CHAPTER II.

THE COLONIAL FLAG.

In the fall of 1775, the Colonial Congress, **then** in session at Philadelphia, appointed Messrs. Franklin, Lynch and Harrison as a committee to consider and recommend a design for a Colonial Flag. General Washington was then in camp at Cambridge, Massachusetts; and the committee went there to consult with him concerning the work in hand.

It was arranged that during their stay in Cambridge, the committeemen were to be entertained by one of the patriotic and well-to-do citizens of the place. This gentleman's residence was one of only modest dimensions; and the front chamber—the "guest chamber," as it was generally called in those days—was already occupied by a very peculiar old gentleman who was a temporary sojourner with the family. This left only one vacant room in the house—a moderate-sized bed-room connecting with the "guest chamber" and also opening into the hall. In order to make room for the Congressional guests, it was arranged that the less transitory occupant would share his apartment with one of them—and it came about, as we will see, that this one was Benjamin Franklin.

Little seems to have been known concerning this

old gentleman; and in the materials from which this account is compiled his name is not even once mentioned, for he is uniformly spoken of or referred to as "the Professor." He was evidently far beyond his three score and ten years ; and he often referred to historical events •of more than a century previous just as if he had been a living witness of their occurrence; still he was erect, vigorous and active—hale, hearty, and clear-minded—as strong and energetic every way as in the mature prime of his life. He was tall, of fine figure, perfectly easy, and very dignified in his manners ; being at once courteous, gracious and commanding. He was, for those times and considering the customs of the Colonists, very peculiar in his method of living; for he ate no flesh, fowl or fish; he never used as food any " green thing," any roots or anything unripe; and he drank no liquor, wine or ale; but confined his diet to cereals and their products, fruits that were ripened on the stem in the sun, nuts, mild tea and the sweets of honey, sugar or molasses. He was well educated, highly cultivated, of extensive as well as varied information, and very studious. He spent considerable of his time in the patient and persistent conning of a number of very rare old books and ancient manuscripts which he seemed to be deciphering, translating or rewriting. These books and manuscripts, together with his own writings, he never showed to any one; and he did not even mention them in his conversations with the family, except in the most casual way; and he always locked them up carefully in a large, old fashioned, cubically shaped, iron bound, heavy, oaken chest, whenever he left his room, even for his meals. He took long and frequent walks alone, sat on the brows of the neighboring hills, or mused in the midst of the green and flower-gemmed meadows. He was fairly liberal —but in no way lavish—in spending his money, with which he was well supplied. He was a quiet, though a very genial and very interesting, member of the family; and he was seemingly at home upon any and every topic coming up in conversation. He was, in short, one whom everyone would notice and respect, whom few would feel well acquainted with, and whom no one would presume to question concerning himself—as to whence he came, why he tarried, or whither he journeyed.

He was firmly, and in a dignified and assured way, one who was in favor of demanding and of securing justice on the part of the Mother Country toward the Colonies. One of his favorite forms of stating the matter was: "We demand no more than our just due; we will accept and be satisfied with nothing less than we demand." Then he would sometimes add: "We demand our rightful dues—justice; and we will soon get all we demand—peaceably, if Parliament is wise—forcibly, if needs be."

The committeemen arrived at Cambridge on the morning of December 13th, and their host invited the General of the Army to dine with them the

same day at his home. When they met for dinner
the party consisted of Washington, the three committeemen, the Professor, the host and the hostess.
The Professor met the guests of his host with an
ease, grace and dignity which was to them all ample
evidence of his superior ability, experience and attainments, and of the propriety of his being among
them—which, however, none of them thought of
questioning. He met the introductions with a
courtly bow, that left no room to doubt that he had
habitually associated with those in acknowledged
authority. When Benjamin Franklin was presented,
however, the latter came forward, extending his
hand, which the Professor heartily accepted; and then
as palm met palm, and as fingers closed upon fingers,
their eyes also met, and there was an instantaneous,
a very apparent and a mutually gratified recognition.

The dinner, of course, followed the usual form of
those days, under similar circumstances ; for even
great men, under the pressure of grave responsibilities, will always at their meals, and especially at a
dining, indulge in commonplace remarks about ordi-
nary affairs. They must, of necessity, repeat or
invent the looked for pleasantries; and they will in
nowise fail to compliment the dishes, the service
and the hostess. In this case, however, conversation soon drifted upon the all-important topic of the
day—the relation of the Colonies to each other and
to the Mother Country, together with the related

question of one's duty to the Colony, as related to
his allegiance to Great Britain; and thence, naturally,
to the work of the Committee—the design for a new
Colonial Flag.

In the discussion of all these topics the Professor
took a noticeable, though not at all an obtrusive, part,
proving himself possessed of a wonderful fund of
varied and accurate information concerning the Colonies, an understanding of their progress, condition
and needs, and a familiarity with the principles and
operations of British and European statesmanship
that was as interesting and instructive to the others
as his earnest patriotism and his assuring confidence
in Colonial success was arousing and encouraging.

The hostess was a very intelligent woman, and an
earnest supporter of all those who demanded justice
for the Colonies, and who were striving to secure
what they demanded; and she took a minor, though
an interested, part in the conversation during the
dinner, especially in relation to the design of a new
flag. She was evidently one of the professor's earnest and intelligent disciples.

As the party were about rising from the table,
there was a brief and undertone consultation between
General Washington and the committeemen, upon
some suggestion to which there seemed to be a ready,
a hearty and an unanimous assent.

· Doctor Franklin then arose, saying, substantially:
"As the chairman of this committee, speaking for
my associates, with their consent, and with the

approval of General Washington, I respectfully invite the Professor to meet with the Committee as one of its members; and we, each one, personally and urgently, request him to accept the responsibility, and to give us, and the American Colonies, the benefit of his presence and his counsel. It has already been arranged that General Washington and our worthy host will also meet with us as honorary members."

The Professor arose, seemingly taller, more erect and more graciously dignified than even his usual wont, saying, in substance:

"I appreciate the compliment bestowed and the honor offered. I humbly accept the invitation, and I cheerfully assume the responsibility of all I may say and do as a co-worker with you. Since, by your unanimous invitation and my unqualified acceptance, I have become a member of your committee, so that I can in all propriety say 'our committee,' I will proceed at once to offer my first suggestion.

"Gentlemen and Comrades, this is a most important occasion. Upon what we do at this time, and at the regular sessions of this committee that will follow this informal and unofficial meeting, there may depend much of the immediate welfare of the people of the Colonies which we represent.

"We are now six—an even number, and not a propitious one for such an enterprise as we have now in hand. We can not spare any one already a member of the committee—even though in so doing we

should improve the conditions in one respect, by
making our number five; but we must needs increase
our number, so we will be seven. This increase of
our numbers should be by the introduction of an element that is usually objected to—or even worse than
objected to, ignored—in all national and political
affairs. I refer to woman—the purifying and intu-
itional element of humanity.

" Let us, therefore, invite our hostess—because she
is our hostess, because she is a woman, and above all,
because she is a superior woman—to become one of
us; and mayhap she will prove a most important
factor in solving the important question which we
are to consider; for more depends on our work here
and now than appears on the surface, to the multi-
tude; and for her patriotism, her intelligence, her
fidelity and her discretion, you may, one and all,
hold me personally and entirely responsible—that
is, if any one of you suppose that any man's indorsement, in any way, adds to an earnest and good
woman's responsibility."

The Professor's first suggestion, as a member of
the committee, was certainly a wonderful innova-
tion, considering the times and the circumstances;
but it was immediately and unanimously adopted.
The hostess was formally invited to become a member of the committee, and she promptly accepted.
She took a somewhat active part in the work of the
committee; for she acted as its secretary; and upon
her notes made at the time, and upon her subsequent

correspondence, this narrative of the committee's operations is mainly based.

The informal session of the committee at the dinner-table adjourned with the understanding that the same seven would meet the same evening, in the same house, in the " guest chamber"—usually occupied by the Professor—there to resume their consideration of a design for a new Colonial Flag.

During the afternoon Franklin and the Professor took a long walk together. They came back apparently well acquainted, and very much pleased with each other. Both of them wore the relieved and confident looks of earnest and determined men who had, in a satisfactory way, solved a perplexing problem, and of victors who had successfully mastered a difficult and dangerous situation. This was so markedly shown in Franklin's face and manner that all the other members of the committee noticed it at the evening session. No one, therefore, was surprised when General Washington asked Doctor Franklin to open the proceedings with such suggestions or recommendations as he had to offer.

Franklin made reply by saying that instead of doing as General Washington desired, he would ask him and the others to listen to his new-found and abundantly honored friend, the Professor, who had very kindly consented to repeat to them, this evening, substantially what he had said to the speaker that afternoon, concerning a new flag for the Colonies, and the reasons for adopting the design which he would submit for their consideration.

FRANKLIN.

Doctor Franklin closed his brief introductory remarks by adding that if the suggested and submitted design for a flag should please the General of the Army and the other members of the committee as fully as it satisfied him, there would be no need of any prolonged session to consider and conclude to recommend the new flag.

Franklin's suggestion was accepted, and the Professor was invited to present his design and the reasons for its adoption. There is no full report of what he said, but the following is an outline of what has been preserved:

"Comrade Americans: We are assembled here to devise and suggest the design for a new flag, which will represent, at once, the principles and determination of the Colonies to unite in demanding and securing justice from the Government to which they still owe recognized allegiance. We are not, therefore, expected to design or recommend a flag which will represent a new government or an independent nation, but one which simply represents the principle that even kings owe something of justice to their loyal subjects. This, I say, is what we are expected to do, because this is the publicly announced, as well as the honestly entertained intent of the great majority of the people of these Colonies, as well as of their representatives in Congress, and of their soldiers in the field. This is unquestionably true *now;* for the sun of our political aim, like the sun in the heavens, is very low in the horizon — just now approaching the winter solstice, which it will reach very soon. But as the sun rises from his grave in Capricorn, mounts toward his resurrection in Aries

and passes onward and upward to his glorious cul-
mination in Cancer, so will our political sun rise and
continue to increase in power, in light and in glory;
and the exalted sun of summer will not have gained
his full strength of heat and power in the starry
Lion until our Colonial Sun will be, in its glorious
exaltation, demanding a place in the governmental
firmament alongside of, coördinate with, and in no
wise subordinate to, any other sun of any other
nation upon earth.

"We are now self-acknowledged Colonies—dependencies of Great Britain, which government we,
as loyal subjects, humbly sue for justice. We will,
ere long, be a self-declared, independent nation,
bestowing upon ourselves the justice for which we
now vainly sue. We must, therefore, design and
recommend a flag which will now recognize our loyalty to Great Britain, and at the same time announce
our earnest and united suit and demand for our
rights as British Subjects.

"These demands will, of course, in the future as
in the past, be neglected or denied. Our justice-
demanding and our freedom-loving companions will
soon learn that there is no hope for us as British
Colonists; and that we can secure the rights we now
contend for—as well as many more, and more to be
prized rights—only as the loyal and united citizens
of a free and an independent American nation.

"General Washington, here, is a British Subject;
aye, he is a British soldier; and he is in command of

British troops; and they are only. attempting to
enforce their rights as loyal subjects of the British
Crown. But General Washington will soon forswear
all allegiance to everything foreign; and he will ere
many months appear before his own people, the
people of these Colonies, and before the world, as the
general commanding the armies of a free and united
people, organized into a new and independent nation.

"The flag which we now recommend must be one
designed and adapted to meet the inevitable—and
soon to be accomplished—change of allegiance. The
flag now adopted must be one that will testify
our present loyalty as English Subjects; and it must
be one easily modified — but needing no radical
change—to make it announce and represent the new
nation which is already gestating in the womb of
time; and which will come to birth—and that not
prematurely, but fully developed and ready for the
change into independent life—before the sun in its
next summer's strength ripens our next harvest.

"The field of our flag must, therefore, be an
entirely new one. For this there are two reasons,
either one of which is amply sufficient why it should
be so. First, the field must be new. because it will
soon represent a new nation. Second, the field must
be one hitherto unused as a national flag; because it
will represent an entirely new principle in government—*the equal rights of man as man.*

"While the field of our flag must be new in the
details of its design, it need not be entirely new in

its elements. It is fortunate for us that there is already in use a flag with which the English Government is familiar, and which it has not only recognized, but also protected for more than half a century, the design of which can be readily modified, or rather extended, so as to most admirably suit our purpose. I refer to the flag of the English East India Company, which is one with a field of alternate longitudinal red and white stripes, and having the Cross of St. George for a union. I, therefore, suggest for your consideration a flag with a field composed of thirteen equally wide, longitudinal, alternate, red and white stripes, and with the Union Flag of England for a union.

"Such a flag can readily be explained to the masses to mean as follows: The Union Flag of the Mother Country is retained as the union of our new flag to announce that the Colonies are loyal to the just and legitimate sovereignty of the British Government. The thirteen stripes will at once be understood to represent the thirteen Colonies; their equal width will type the equal rank, rights and responsibilities of the Colonies. The union of the stripes in the field of our flag will announce the unity of interests and the coöperative union of efforts, which the Colonies recognize and put forth in their common cause. The white stripes will signify that we consider our demands just and reasonable; and that we will seek to secure our rights through peaceable, intelligent and statesmanlike means—if they prove at all possible; and the red stripes at the top and bottom of our flag will declare that first and last—and always—we have the determination, the enthusiasm, and the power to use force, whenever we deem force necessary. The alternation of the red and white stripes will suggest that our reasons for all demands will be intelligent and forcible, and that our force in securing our rights will be just and reasonable. All this is in strict accordance with the present public sentiment in the Colonies; for, as I have already said, the masses of the people, and a large majority of the leaders of public opinion, desire a removal of grievances, and a rectification of wrongs, through a fuller recognition of their rights as British Subjects; and few of them desire, and very few of them expect—at this time—any complete severance of their present political and dependent relations with the English Government.

"There are other weightier and eternal reasons for a flag having the field I suggest; but it will be time enough to consider them when, in the near future, we, or our successors, are considering—not a temporary flag for associated and dependent Colonies but—a permanent standard for a united and an independent nation. Thanking you, one and all, for your complimentary courtesy and for your patient attention, I submit this miniature drawing of the suggested flag for your intelligent consideration."

The remarks of the Professor made a most profound impression; and the design which he submitted was, in every particular, satisfactory to every one present.   It was enthusiastically endorsed, General Washington and Doctor Franklin giving it especial approval and unstinted praises.

It was formally and unanimously adopted; and shortly before midnight the Committee adjourned. The 13th of December, 1775, therefore, witnessed the presentation, consideration and approval of the only official flag of the Coöperating American Colonies;

THE COLONIAL FLAG.

and the extreme probability is that until that time a flag with a field of alternate red and white stripes, much less a field of thirteen stripes, had never been made or seen in the American Colonies.

There is no record of any congressional action upon the report of this committee; nor, indeed, any record of any report made by the committee. This design was, however, adopted by General Washington as the general flag and recognized standard of the Colonial Army and Navy.

A full sized garrison flag was, as speedily as possible, made in strict accordance with the drawing presented by the Professor.

On January 2, 1776, at Cambridge, in the presence of the military, with the assistance of his officers, and with appropriate ceremonies—in which the Franklin Committee were participants—General Washington, with his own hands, hoisted the newly accepted and newly made banner upon a towering and specially raised pine tree liberty pole ; thus unfurling to the breeze and displaying to his army, the citizens of the vicinity, and the British forces in Boston, for the first time, the new and officially recognized Confederated Colonial Flag.

This was the first authoritative recognition of any standard having the color of Congressional action as a distinctively accepted flag to represent the confederated and coöperative union of the Colonies in their resistance of tyranny, injustice and oppression.   And this was the first time in the history of the world when thirteen alternate red and white stripes was the foundation field of any national standard.

When this flag was first displayed at Cambridge, it was clearly seen by the British officers at Charlestown Heights, who, with the aid of their field glasses, easily made out all the details of its design and construction.   These officers, in their wonderful wisdom. interpreted the raising of this flag—which they said " is thoroughly English, you know "—to mean that

General Washington thus announced his surrender
to them ; and they, at once, saluted "The Thirteen
Stripes" with thirteen hearty cheers; and they immediately followed this spontaneous outburst of
British Enthusiasm with the grander and more dignified official salute of thirteen guns.

This unintended official recognition, and this
"baptism in fire" of the newly adopted Colonial Flag
by its enemies—who thirteen times filled the air
with their cheering acclaims, and who thirteen times
burned the sweet and pungent incense of their military "God speed you" in the presence of its first
official "unfurling to the light," was one of the
most singular, most mysterious and most prophetic
procedures of Revolutionary days.

It was indeed a prophecy Divine—
That light of grand success should ever shine
In gloried brightness, and in matchless might,
Upon this flag of Justice, Truth and Right.

The Colonial military forces on land and the naval
vessels at sea did not immediately, or even soon,
uniformly adopt the "Stripes and Union" of the
Franklin Committee. The troops of the different
Colonies still—on frequent occasions at least—carried the colors of their own commonwealth or of
their own local organization. The same was also
true as to the navy, privateers and merchant vessels.

The three flags most frequently spoken of, however, and evidently most common, and all of which

HISTORIAN'S OFFICE

Church of Jesus Christ of Latter-day Saints

47 East South Temple St.

SALT LAKE CITY, UTAH

were recognized as representing the Colonies **as** united for mutual coöperative military operations, were the "Stars and Union." and some modification or combination of the Pine Tree and Rattle Snake

JOHN PAUL JONES.

banners.   Mention is also made of a red flag, with thirteen alternate red and white stripes forming the union.   Another banner—which is said to have been carried at the Battle of White Plains October 28,

WHITE PLAINS FLAG.

1776 — is described as one with a white field, in which is a crossed sword and staff — the latter being surmounted by a "Liberty Cap;" above which design the flag also bears the then not uncommon motto, "Liberty or Death."

A dark red flag, with the motto "LIBERTY," was carried by the Americans at the Battle of Long Island, August 26, 1776.

That there was no generally recognized Colonial Standard is evident from the frequent use of so many different flags, even after the Declaration of Independence. This is also confirmed into a certainty by many official and private letters of the army and naval officers written during 1775 and 1776, in which they described the colors they carried on certain occasions; and frequently ask what colors they are to display; or ask for designs so that they may procure such flags as are appropriate.

The Colonial Legislature—or Congress, as it was then called—of Georgia gave official recognition to the " Stripes and Union" very soon after its display at Cambridge; and the Convention of Virginia unfurled the new flag over its deliberations officially in May, 1776.

Lieutenant John Paul Jones claims that he had the distinguished honor of hoisting the " Flag of America" the first time it was displayed by a Conti nental man-of-war vessel?

The Declaration of Independence, at Philadelphia, on July 4, 1776, transformed the hitherto British Colonies into Independent States; changed the Colonial Congress into as nearly a Continental Legislature as under the circumstances it could become; and made John Hancock the representative head of the new government. The Colonial Flag, of "Thirteen Stripes and British Union," thus became

JOHN HANCOCK.

the Standard of the thirteen newly nationalized and coöperating state governments.

The Continental Flag was first hoisted East of the Atlantic by the Captain of the Reprisal.

The first salute of the Continental Flag, by a foreign power (after the one by the British Forces at Charlestown Heights) was to the one displayed by the Andrea Doria, at St. Eustatia, November 16.1776.

CHAPTER III.

THE STARS AND STRIPES.

The officially recorded history of the adoption of the Stars and Stripes as the flag of the Thirteen United States* is precise and pointed, but it is very brief. The entire official information upon this most interesting subject is contained in one sentence of the Journal of the Continental Congress, and it reads as follows:

"*Resolved*, That the flag of the thirteen United States be thirteen stripes alternate red and white; and that the union be thirteen stars, white, in a blue field, representing a new constellation."

This resolution was passed by the Congress, at Philadelphia, on June 14, 1777. It was nearly a year after the Declaration of Independence, and a year and a half after the meeting of the Franklin Committee on the Colonial Flag, at Cambridge, that the English Union in the American flag was replaced by the blue field containing thirteen stars. Even

---

*It should be borne in mind that the adoption of the Stars and Stripes as the flag of the "Thirteen United States" did not make that flag a National Standard. There was, at that time, thirteen former Colonies which had declared themselves each an independent State; but there was no governmental union of these States. They were associated together by a very vaguely understood compact, improperly defined as a Continental League or

after this Congressional action there was much delay in making it known. The newspapers of the day did not notice the matter for six or eight weeks, and the official birth of the Stars and Stripes was not formally announced by the Secretary of Congress

Confederation. There was no President, Cabinet or Senate; no National Legislature or Treasury. Each State had its own Congress, its own administration, its own army and its own currency; and some of them even charged custom duties on goods imported from the other States. Each State obeyed only such laws of the Continental or Confederation Congress as its own Congress chose to accept and ratify. In short, the Legislative body, which met at Philadelphia and which was called a Congress, was simply an Advisory Council, made up of representatives from the different States; and it had no power over the purse or sword of any State or citizen. Even when the final treaty of peace was signed at Versailles, on September 3, 1783, the independence and the individual nationality of the thirteen States, each by its own proper name, was separately recognized; and there was, in that document, no intimation of their union or even their confederation as a single nation.

The States were held together more by outside pressure, which necessitated coöperative efforts in mutual defense, than by any fraternal feeling—or national sentiment. The inadequacy of such a loosely formed Confederation was very soon recognized, and the spirit of national union rapidly developed; for every step in governmental theory, and every actual change in administration, was toward the idea of "An empire of free republics indissolubly united."

This idea became an accomplished fact upon the inauguration of the new government, in 1789. Up to that date the Stars and Stripes formed the flag of the " *Thirteen United States.*" Since that time the " Red, White and Blue " has been the National Standard of the UNITED STATES OF AMERICA.

until eighty-one days later—on September 3d, following.

There is no official record of any committee having been appointed by Congress to consider this matter, nor of any designs for a National Standard having been submitted or suggested; nor of any explanations offered; nor of any arguments used; nor of any remarks made—nor, indeed, of any vote taken in connection with the adoption of the design of Our Flag—the Stars and Stripes.

This remarkable meagerness in the official record, in connection with one of the most important items of legislation ever considered by the "American People of the Thirteen States in Congress Assembled," is most convincing proof of a thorough and conclusive consideration of the whole matter by the leading statesmen of those times before its presentation for Congressional action. The truth seems to be that the prompt decision of this interesting and important question by the National Legislature was simply the formal and the official ratification of what had already been fully, though informally, agreed upon by all who took an active interest therein.

Admiral Preble in his voluminous, exhaustive and most valuable work, "The History of the Flag of the United States," says: "No record of the discussions which must have preceded the adoption of the Stars and Stripes has been preserved, and we do not know to whom we are indebted for their beauti-

ful and soul inspiring devices. * * * * There
are many theories of its origin, but though less than
a century (at the time he wrote) has elapsed none
are satisfactory."

The origin of the colors red, white and blue, have
been supposably traced to several different sources.
Some have found the antecedents for our stripes in
the Dutch Flag elsewhere spoken of and described.
One theory is that they were borrowed from Washington's Coat of Arms; but there is for this only a
very slim foundation, and it is not now seriously
considered. The British East India Company's flag
has been referred to and described as an antetype
suggestive of the Stripes and Union or Continental
Standard. There have been innumerable theories
as to the origin of the blue color in the union and of
the white stars placed therein. Many of these
theories are very suggestive ; some of them wonder-
fully ingenious, and each one of them is, of course,
more or less plausible. One writer is eloquent in
these words: " Every nation has its symbolic ensign
Some have beasts, some birds, some fishes, some rep-
tiles on their banners. Our fathers chose the Stars
and Stripes—the red telling of the blood shed by
them for their country, the blue telling of the
heavens and their protection, and the stars announcing the different States embodied in one nationality,
E Pluribus Unum."

There is a very plausible claim that a flag of
thirteen alternate red and white stripes with a blue

union containing thirteen white stars, was made by
Mrs. John Ross, of Philadelphia, in June, 1776. This
flag is said to have been made from a design drawn
by General Washington with some important
changes suggested by Mrs. Ross. The probability is
that there is a mistake of a year in this matter; and
that Mrs. Ross made her flag in 1777.

There are quite a number of paintings, portraits
and battle scenes, as well as many old engravings,
which indicate that the Stars and Stripes were in use
as a flag during 1775 and 1776. These paintings and
engravings were all, however, executed after—and
most of them *several years after* Congressional action
upon the National Standard—when the new and
immediately popular flag had become familiar.
Painters and poets are not generally noted for their
historical accuracy—especially when every natural
feeling of the painter, the sitter for a portrait, and
the patron of a picture would naturally incline
towards the beautiful, novel and glorious National
Standard wherever it would be at all admissible.

The simple fact seems to be that the Stars and
Stripes were never used as a flag until after their
official adoption by Congress. Only a few individuals had ever thought of the design in that or any
other connection until a short time before it was presented to and accepted by the Representatives of the
American People in Congress assembled on June 14,
1777.

From the same source that furnishes the history of

the origin of the Colonial Flag there is also much to be learned concerning the origin, the meaning, the informal consideration and the reason to be, of the final adoption of the Stars and Strips as the National Standard.

It seems that after the adjournment of the Franklin Committee at Cambridge, on the evening of December 13, 1775, Doctor Franklin, General Washington and the Professor, spent most of the night in earnest comparison of views concerning the momentous question in which they each and all had such vital interest.

They all agreed that the proper policy to pursue was to press vigorously and persistently the demands of the Colonists for the redress of all their wrongs, and the full recognition of their rights, as British Subjects. Franklin and Washington had fair hopes of success on this line of procedure; the Professor none at all. Still the latter was heartily in favor of pressing the demands upon the English Government; and they were all of one mind in believing that the continued refusal or neglect of the Home Government to comply with such just demands would speedily ripen and popularize the sentiment and the ideas of the Colonists into an enthusiasm and determination toward a confederation of the Colonies as independent States; and the Professor confidently maintained that such a result would surely be accomplished within the coming year, with the two gentlemen before him as important factors in the formation and establishment of the New Government. He informed them also that he had some suggestions concerning, and an appropriate design for, the flag of the New American Nation—so soon to take its place among the recognized governments of the world; and he added that these suggestions and this design would be forthcoming at the proper time and place—when such flag was under consideration as a practical issue.

The following memoranda is in the handwriting of the lady who made the notes of the Franklin Committee-meeting in Cambridge, and in the same hand bears this endorsement:

"By direction of Dr. Franklin, now in Paris, I made this copy of the Professor's memoranda; and to-day I delivered the original of the same, and also a sealed letter (marked " private " and tied up with it), into the hands of General Washington. May 13, 1777."

The following scrap in the same handwriting, and evidently from a letter—but showing neither date, address nor signature—is full of suggestion:

"You know how much interest I have taken in the new flag. It seems that there has been considerable attention given to the matter, in a quiet way, by some of our prominent men; and that the Professor's design is almost universally pleasing to them. Last Friday afternoon I was invited to be present at a little gathering where the subject would be considered ; and you may be sure I was greatly surprised, and not a little confused, to find myself the only woman there, while there was of men a round dozen. They read the Professor's memoranda and discussed the design. That is they one and all approved it. I explained to them how I came to be the custodian of the paper, and why they had not been sooner delivered to General Washington. The matter is finally settled, however, for the very next day the Congress here adopted the Stars and Stripes as the flag of the thirteen Colonies. And now that the matter is brought to such a satisfactory issue, you can not, I am sure, at all imagine how pleased I am with the result, and how proud I am with the accidental and humble part I have had in its consummation."

This letter evidently refers to a meeting held on the afternoon of Friday, June 13, 1777, the day before congressional action upon and the adoption of the Stars and Stripes.

MEMORANDA.

A Flag for the New American Nation, to be formed by the Union of the thirteen Independent States in America.

COLORS.—Three; Red, White and Blue.

FIELD.—Same as the Colonial Flag; that is, thirteen stripes of equal width, Red and White, alternately.

UNION.—Blue; in depth equal to seven stripes, containing thirteen white stars, five-pointed, one point up.

POPULAR INTERPRETATION.

COLORS.—*Red*, signifies war, if necessary *White*, arbitration, intelligence, justice. *Blue*, is industry and economy.

THIRTEEN STRIPES.-- Suggest the thirteen Colonies united in one nation for common defense and mutual assistance.

THE BLUE FIELD.—Will represent the overarching sky, in which the thirteen stars form a new, a glorious and a permanent constellation.

MYSTIC MEANING AND ESOTERIC INTERPRETATION
OF THE
NEW FLAG—THE STARS AND STRIPES.

The flag of a nation should be the symbol of the ideal upon which the nation is founded, and this

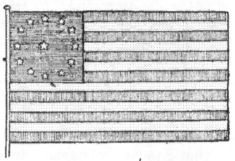

ORIGINAL STARS AND STRIPES.

must always be the ideal of manhood, as that ideal is conceived of by the founders of the nation. This is true, because every possible organization among men is, in accordance with the theory of such organization, in the form of a man. In other words, every organization among men, so far as the principles and purposes, the operations and results, of such organization is concerned, is simply a man who is in size the sum total of all men in the organization, and who in form is the collated aggregates of their recognized ideal man.

The ideal nation, therefore, must be in the form of the ideal man—with all the recognized characteristics of the ideal man as to rights, duties, purposes, methods of operation and destiny. It naturally follows that one's conception of the ideal man simply needs enlargement to constitute his conception of the ideal nation. When, therefore, one has determined the appropriate design to symbolize his conception of the ideal man, he has also found the appropriate design for the Flag of his ideal nation.

The Stars and Stripes, as above described, are the appropriate elements for the flag of our new ideal nation, because they are the complete and beautiful symbols of the characteristics of the ideal man.

A few suggestions as to the different forms of government will illustrate what is meant by the ideal nation, the ideal government and the ideal man.

THEOCRACY values men as the material out of which to manufacture unnumbered hosts of glorifying worshipers, who will pay abject homage and unquestioning obedience to the recognized " Theos," or to his priestly or royal vice-gerents.

AUTOCRACY estimates men as the inherited or accumulated capital to be used in ministering to the ease and comfort, the pleasure and the ambition, of the ruler who holds his subjects, even in life or death, as the means of gratifying his settled purposes or his transitory whims. Both Theocracy and Autocracy

are based upon the fundamental false idea of absolute ownership and domination—power without
responsibility—on the part of the ruler, and of abject
obedience, without modification, delay or question,
on the part of the subjects. Government is considered as of the Sovereign, by the Sovereign and for
Sovereign, without any such idea as the subject having any rights or duties, except as he is of service to
the ruler.

ARISTOCRACY appreciates a limited number of
equals, in rank and rights, for their co-operation and
assistance in maintaining their dominion over the
masses; and, like Autocracy, values and appreciates
all of inferior rank for their lack of rights, except
the right to be useful as servants, supporters and
defenders of the superior or aristocratic few.

DEMOCRACY estimates men by parties and by
majorities. It values men for their fixedness of
habit in clinging to the traditions of the past, which
insures that they will continue their plodding work
in the well worn party harness, thus perpetuating
the rule of the party in power, thus continuing the
dominition of the recognized party leaders—through
the grinding operation of party machinery. The
party out of power values men for their restlessness
and discontent; for their susceptibility under an
appeal to some real or fancied wrong, to join the
opposition which aims to dethrone the leaders in
office and turn the government over to the " outs "—
who thus become the " ins."

A REPUBLIC is simply a democracy with modified methods of detail in the administration of the government.

All these forms of government have, heretofore, been organized upon the fundamental false assumption that the man who is strong of arm or superior in the accident of rank or intelligence, has the natural or (as it is sometimes called) the Divine right to dominate absolutely, for his own purposes, and by such methods as he may choose, all other men who are weaker in muscle or who are less intelligent or less self-assertive; and that consequently the masses have few if any rights which the one who is stronger or wiser is bound to respect. In short the principle of government has, heretofore, been that might— whether of brawn or will—gives the right to absolute and unquestionable dominition; and that lighter physique or weaker will is the sin that bears the natural penalty of abject and unquestioning servitude. Our new National Government is founded upon the declaration. "All men are born free; and every man has an equal right to life, liberty and happiness." This is at least the negative side of philanthropy; because it recognizes the equal rights of man as man—of every individual man; and it impliedly suggests willing and chosen coöperation, instead of arbitrary dominition and enforced obedience.

PHILANTHROPY looks at man in the singular number; and it estimates man individually. Philanthropy aims to render man virtuous rather than obedient. It seeks to lead man into holiness rather than to inculcate obligation.

PHILANTHROPY fosters intelligence rather than the impartation of traditional rules; and it stimulates individual, productive usefulness, rather than the enforcing of habitual, routine drudgery. Philanthropy aspires to develop each man into a "king," who will purely and wisely rule himself; and into a "priest" who will commune with the highest and make his life one of practical purity. Philanthropy aims and endeavors to elevate and perfect humanity by arousing, teaching and assisting each individual man to perfect himself.

Now the Stars and Stripes symbolize man, the philanthropic man, the man who is aspiring to, planning for, and developing in all that renders him a more perfect human being.

THE COLORS.—Red is the symbol of man in the realm of his desires, his impulses, his yearnings and his aspirations. As Red is shaded and darkened it types the sensual and the selfish nature in man, and it then symbolizes impurity, dishonesty, injustice and tyranny. As Red is tinted and lightened toward the more delicate shades of pink it types tenderness, gentleness, affection tinged with weakness; and thus impractical sentimentality. The Clear Red types that ardent and pure love which is at once kind and courageous. It symbolizes that manly philanthropy which aspires to the greatest good of the individual

man, and thus of the entire race, and that will strive
for that end regardless of whether the path lie in
the well worn highway — with consequent smooth
traveling — or whether it must encounter fatigue,
opposition and temporary discomfiture.

White is the symbol of man in the intellectual
domain; and it represents wisdom, intelligence, know-
ledge, healthful imagination, clear intuition and cor-
rect thinking; and it, therefore, symbolizes justice.
Blue is the type of man in the realm of his physical
existence and operation. It therefore refers to
man's physical well being, his activities and his productive usefulness — to his condition, welfare and
success in actual development, as manifested in the
phenomenal world. The Red and White, in alternate
equal stripes, teach that in all man's life and work
the pure purpose and the wise plan must be equal
factors; and these factors must be coördinate and
constant; that purity and intelligence are the essence
and form of every successful operation that finds its
outworking and resulting effect in the blue field of
man's practical life and manifestation. The three
Red and the three White alternate stripes, that
run the full length of the flag, symbolize the
beautiful truth that aspiration and intelligence,
affection and thought, purpose and plan, will and
system, must be the grand underlying, general and
comprehensive factors in the whole of every pure,
true and useful life ; and that this must be the case

in each of the three planes of man's life—the moral, the intellectual and the physical.

The seven short alternate Red and White stripes opposite the Blue field refer to the particulars and details of man's life. The Red stripe at the base of these seven, and opposite the lower margin of the Blue field, signifies that every special purpose, plan and activity should have a pure and philanthropic foundation; while the Red stripe at the top alludes to the special superior and perfecting human quality attained by the individual, and through the individual by the race, by such constant, loving, wise and useful endeavor. The short, alternate, Red and White stripes opposite the Blue field particularize the teachings of the full-length stripes; that is they announce and emphasize the idea that the special and temporary purposes, plans and activities of every day's operations, like the grand aspiration, theory and effort of one's life, should be pure, intelligent and effective—and at the same time harmonious and mutually coöperative—on the three planes of will, intellect, and experience; in short that the ideal aim and object of the whole life of man should also be the special aim and object of every particular subsidiary purpose, plan and act.

As the Blue field symbolizes man in the realm of physical existence and productive manifestation, the White stars therein will readily and beautifully symbolize the definite and special attainments in which his ideal aspirations and his actual developments are fully unified, or harmoniously adjusted. The five-pointed star, one point up, symbolizes the man whose philanthropic purpose is clearly and fully defined in a dynamic will that is intelligently, absolutely and unchangeably determined. He who has a pure purpose which transcends all others, an intelligent plan which includes all others, with an exalted and unswerving determination that utilizes all minor operations, and who is devoting his whole being and life to accomplish his grand purpose, is appropriately represented by the pentagram, one point up.

The Thirteen Stripes, while they will for a long time—and perhaps always—very well represent the number of Colonies which unite their interests, their efforts and their governmental destinies in the formation of the first independent nation in America, have yet a very beautiful and a very important, and a much deeper meaning.

Thirteen is, according to the initiating instruction of the Ancient Magi, the number of "Progress Perpetuity, and Perfection." There were twelve tribes of the Children of Israel—but Moses, the thirteenth, was the one who ruled and directed them all; or the Levites, the priestly, and, therefore, the most honorable of them all, may be numbered as the Thirteenth. There were twelve disciples in the Apostolic College; but Jesus, its founder and the enlightener, was over them all, and he was the Thirteenth. There are twelve gates to the Holy City of the Apocalypse; but the grand avenue of Divine influx

from above, without which the other twelve would
be only gates to eternal darkness, is the Thirteenth.
There are twelve signs in the Zodiac; the sum total
of them all is the surrounding firmament, in the center of which is the Thirteenth, the illuminating and
sustaining Sun. There are twelve months in the
year, which in their aggregate and union, form the
year, which is the Thirteenth. All the ill omens
ever attached to the number Thirteen are simply
suggestions of the retribution which overtakes those
who profane that which is essentially sacred.

Thirteen as applied to man symbolizes the natural man whose instinctive and selfish impulses are
being regenerated into harmonious and coöperative
perfection with his ideal aspirations. It, therefore,
symbolizes the actualizing of the ideally perfected
family, church or nation, which is founded upon and
developing upon the grand truths of the Absolute
Fatherhood of the Divine and the consequent Universal Brotherhood of Man.

In short, then, the Stars and Stripes symbolize
the man who, with a pure heart, clear brain and
working hands, is philanthropically, intelligently and
successfully, step by step, realizing his aspirations
in developing continually into a higher and holier
ideal, Divine Manhood.

As the flag of our nation, the Stars and Stripes
will symbolize a philanthropic government founded
upon these principles, administered in accordance
with these theories, and, therefore, accomplishing for

its individual citizens, and thus through them for the
race, the glorious result of a perfected humanity—
bound together in an ideal and an actual Brotherhood of Man.

Benjamin Franklin, who took so prominent a
part in all Colonial affairs, including the adoption of
the design for the Colonial Flag, was not in this
country when the Stars and Stripes were officially
chosen as the Flag of the Nation. He was, however, devoting all his wonderful abilities to the service of his country, in securing its recognition at the
Court of France, and in securing also the practical
assistance of that powerful government. As illus-
trating his simple manners, great ability and most
wonderful personal popularity, the following anec-
dote is introduced :

When Franklin was received at the French
Court as American Minister, he felt some scruples of
conscience in complying with their fashions as to
dress. "He hoped," he said to the minister, "that
as he was himself a very plain man, and represented
a plain republican people, the king would indulge
his desire to appear at court in his usual dress.
Independent of this, the season of the year, he said,
rendered the change from warm yarn stockings to
fine silk somewhat dangerous."

The French Minister made him a bow, but said
that the fashion was too sacred a thing for him to
meddle with, but he would do himself the honor to
mention it to his majesty.

The King smiled, and returned word that Franklin was welcome to appear at Court in any dress he pleased. In spite of that delicate respect for strangers, for which the French are so remarkable, the courtiers could not help staring, at first, at Franklin's Quaker-like dress, and especially at his "Blue Yarn Stockings." But it soon appeared as though he had been introduced upon this splendid theatre only to demonstrate that great genius, like true beauty, "needs not the foreign aid of ornament." The Court were so dazzled by the brilliancy of his mind that they never looked at his stockings.

Lieutenant John Paul Jones, who was placed in command of the Ranger on the same day that Congress adopted the Stars and Stripes, was probably the first one to hoist the new National Flag over a United States war vessel, by placing it at the main-top of the Ranger in Portsmouth harbor.

The Stars and Stripes were first saluted by a foreign naval power—thus recognizing the independence of the United States—on February 14, 1778. This occurred in French waters, when Admiral LaMotte Piquet, of the French navy, returned the salute of Lieutenant Jones.

The Stars and Stripes were probably first unfurled over the United States Military forces at Fort Stanwix—afterward Fort Schuyler—the site of which is now occupied by the town of Rome, on August 2, 1777. The Fort was invested, and the garrison—being without colors—proceeded to manufacture a standard. They cut up their shirts to furnish the white material for stripes and stars; the blue they took from the cloak of one of the officers, and the red was obtained in smaller pieces from different officers and soldiers. The flag thus completed was displayed with enthusiasm and many cheers, and the remnants of this mosaic flag would have been as gallantly defended and as precious in the eyes of that garrison as would have been any silk and gold standard ever manufactured.

The Battle of Brandywine is the first occasion when it is certain that the Stars and Stripes were displayed at any military engagement—on September 11, 1777.

From this time on the Stars and Stripes were generally adopted, and everywhere recognized as the Standard Flag of the new nation.

The Stars and Stripes first floated over a foreign and captured fort at Nassau, January 28, 1778.

The United States formed her first treaty of alliance with France, and it was signed at Paris, February 6, 1778. The army, under Washington, celebrated this event by a very peculiar demonstration. After a review of the Army by the Commanding General—every one decked out in his best, with every piece of bunting floating, and with an unprecedented enthusiasm—there was a salute of thirteen guns, a full discharge of musketry, and a rousing cheer of "Long live the King of France!" Again there were thirteen guns and the general discharge of musketry, with the "Huzza! Long live the friendly European Powers!" Finally there was a repetition of the thirteen guns and the general discharge of musketry, with the "Huzza for the United States!"

When the officers mustered for the refreshment of the inner man, they came to the tables thirteen abreast. linking arms to indicate that the Thirteen States were in fellowship and union.

It is not certainly known, from any authentic or official information, who first displayed the Stars and Stripes in a British port. The claim for this honor has been made for several different vessels and their captains. Commodore Preble, who has given the matter careful and extended examination, is of the opinion that this distinction belongs to Captain William Moores, of the Bedford, from Nantucket, who raised the American Standard over his vessel, at London, February 3, 1783.

Captain John Green, of the Empress, was probably the first to display the Stars and Stripes in China—in 1784.

The Columbia, Captain John Kendrick, sailed from Boston in the fall of 1787. She passed around Cape Horn in January, 1788—spending the summer on the northwest coast of North America. She sailed thence to China, and returned via the Cape of Good Hope, and arrived in Boston in 1790. This was the first time the Stars and Stripes were carried around the world.

Singular as it may appear, the first bloc
upon foreign soil in any battle under the Stars anu
Strips was in Ireland. More singular still, the
melee was one in which the British Soldier fought,
not under the Union Flag of England, but under the
Stars and Stripes of America.

Lemuel Cox, an eminent American engineer,
built a bridge of American Oak over the River Foyle
at Londonderry. When the bridge was nearly completed he opened it in a complimentary way to the
use of the citizens; and he very naturally raised over
it the Stars and Stripes of his own nation. Finding
that the loitering throng of visitors interfered with
his workmen, he closed the gates at either end of the
bridge to keep out the crowd. A mob ensued, which
the mayor and military came out to disperse. It
thus happened that the British army, at Londonderry, in Ireland, on November 22, 1790, fought
their first, last and—thus far—their only battle under
the Stars and Stripes; killing three and wounding
several in the encounter.

The first salute by an English war-vessel to the
Stars and Stripes occurred at Boston, on May 2,
1791, when Captain Isaac Coffin, of the British
man-of-war Alligator, recognized the American
Standard with thirteen guns as he entered the
harbor. The salute was, of course, immediately
responded to by the fortress at the Castle.

Vermont was admitted into the Union as a State,
on March 4, 1791, and Kentucky came into the

sisterhood June 1, 1792. The flag of thirteen stripes and thirteen stars did not, therefore, represent the number of States. Congress on January 7, 1794, took up the matter of altering the flag so as to make it conform to the changed condition of affairs. The matter called up much discussion and considerable ill feeling; but a bill changing the flag to one of fifteen stripes and fifteen stars—the change to be made May 1st, next ensuing—was passed, and the President approved it, January 13, 1794.

The American Flag was, therefore, one of fifteen stripes and fifteen stars from May 1, 1794, until the next change, which took place July 4, 1818.

The French National Convention on August 15, 1794, decreed that their own National Tricolor and the Stars and Stripes should be suspended from the vault of their Assembly Hall in Paris, " as a sign of perpetual alliance and union." Mr. Monroe, who was then United States minister to France, presented the Convention with the Stars and Stripes, for that purpose; and the two Standards were accordingly displayed together, in the Assembly Hall of the French Nation.

Mr. Adel, the French minister to the United States, on January 1, 1796, presented to the United States Government the French National Tricolor. The ceremony took place with much pomp and detail—President Washington accepting the colors on behalf of Congress and the American people.

The Betsey, a little ninety-ton ship, Captain

Edmund Fanning, sailed from New York, in 1797, and was the first vessel to carry the Fifteen Stars and Stripes around the world.

The Stars and Stripes were first displayed at Natchez, Mississippi, over territory recently acquired by treaty from Spain on February 29, 1797.

The Stars and Stripes were first unfurled at Constantinople in 1800. The authorities there were in total ignorance of any such nation as the United States, but upon learning a new lesson in geography they gave to Captain Bainbridge and his Banner a cordial welcome—and he soon became a prime favorite with the Mussulmans.

The American Flag was first raised over a captured Fortress, east of the Atlantic, on April 27, 1805, when the Tripolitan Fort Derne was thus adorned—after hauling down the native flag.

The admission of new States into the Union again rendered the flag of fifteen stars and fifteen stripes out of harmony with the number of States in the nation.

Congress appointed a committee " to inquire into the expediency of altering the flag of the United States." On January 2, 1817, this committee made the following report:

" That they have maturely examined the subject submitted to their consideration, and we are well aware that any proposition essentially to alter the flag of the United States, either in the general form or in the distribution of its parts, would be as unacceptable to the Legislature and to the people, as it would be uncongenial with the views of the committee.

"Fully persuaded that the form selected for the American flag was truly emblematical of our origin and existence, as an independent nation, and that, as such, it has received the approbation and support of the citizens of the Union, it ought to undergo no change that would decrease its conspicuity or tend to deprive it of its representative character. The committee, however, believe that a change in the number of States in the Union sufficiently indicates the propriety of such a change in the arrangement of the flag as shall best accord with the reason that led to its adoption, and sufficiently points to important periods of our history.

" * * * * The certain prospect that at no distant day the number of States will be considerably multiplied renders it, in the opinion of the committee, highly inexpedient to increase the number of stripes, as every flag must, in some measure, be limited in its size, from the circumstance of convenience to the place on which it is to be displayed, while such an increase would necessarily decrease their magnitude, and render them proportionally less distinct to distant observation. * * * *

" The national flag being in general use, it appears to the committee of considerable importance to adopt some arrangement calculated to prevent, in future, great or extensive alterations. Under these impressions, they are led to believe no alteration could be more emblematic of our origin and present existence, as composed of a number of independent and united States, than to reduce the stripes to the original thirteen—representing the number of States then contending for, and happily achieving their independence; and to increase the stars to correspond with the number of States now in the Union; and hereafter to add one star to the flag whenever a new State shall be fully admitted.

    *   *   *   *   *   *

" The committee cannot believe that, in retaining only thirteen stripes, it follows that they refer to certain individual States, inasmuch as nearly all the new States were a component part of, and represented in, the original; and inasmuch, also, as the flag is intended to signify numbers, and not local and particular sections of the Union."

No action was taken upon this report at that session of Congress. The matter was, however, brought up again at the next session on December 17, 1817. It was discussed from time to time in Congress, and frequently considered among the members, military men and citizens. Mr. Wendover, who had charge of the bill, and who worked industriously to have it passed, writes on March 24, 1818:

" This day the first call on the docket was the Star-Spangled Banner. I moved to go into committee on the bill. General Smith moved to discharge the committee of the whole, and postpone the bill indefinitely. I appealed to that gentleman and the House, if they were willing thus to neglect the banner of freedom.

" General Smith's motion was negatived by almost a unanimous vote, and we hoisted the striped bunting in committee of the whole. After I had made a few observations and sat down, Mr. Poindexter moved to strike out *twenty* stars and insert *seven*, with a view to have the stripes for the old and the stars for the new states. Motion rejected nearly unanimously. Mr. Folger then moved to strike out *twenty* and insert thirteen—to restore the original flag; his motion was also negatived by a similar vote. Mr. Robertson then expressed a wish to fix an arbitrary number of stripes, say nine or eleven; but no one seemed to approve of his idea, and the committee rose and reported the bill without amendment; and the House ordered it to be engrossed for a third reading to-morrow, by almost a unanimous vote.   *   *   *

" P. S. March 25th.

" The bill had its third reading this day, a little before twelve o'clock, and passed with perhaps two or three noes."

The bill as passed is as follows :

" An Act To Establish the Flag of The United States.

" Section 1. *Be it enacted, etc.* That from and after the Fourth day of July next, the flag of the United States be thirteen horizontal stripes alternate red and white; that the Union have twenty stars, white in a blue field.

"Section 2. *And be it further enacted,* That on the admission of every new State into the Union, one star be added to the Union of the flag; and that such addition shall take effect on the Fourth of July next succeeding such admission.

"Approved April 4, 1818."

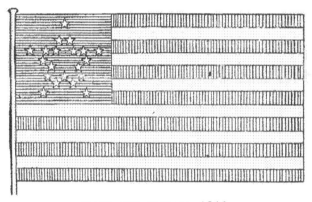

STARS AND STRIPES, 1818.

The flags of the United States are now constructed under this law.

The first flag raised under this enactment was one made at the request of Mr. P. H. Wendover, M. C., by Mrs. S. C. Reid, of New York, with the assistance of her husband, who was among the earliest and ablest advocates of such a flag. The stars in this flag were arranged so as to form a large five-pointed star, co-centric with the Union.

This standard was displayed over the House of Representatives on April 14, 1818. This was only ten days after the approval of the Act; and it was nearly three months before such a flag had any legal existence or value.

There has never been any action of Congress to determine in what manner the stars should be arranged in the Union; and the result is an innumerable number of designs—according to the taste, fancy or whim of whoever may choose to dispose of the stars in the National Constellation. The size and proportion of the flag is not determined by Congressional action, but by the Army and Naval Departments of the Government.

NAVAL FLAGS.

The Navy Department on May 18, 1818, directed that the Standard Flag should be, in accordance

* * * * *
  * * * * *
* * * * *
  * * * * *

with the above law, with the stars arranged like the accompanying diagram.

The flag was to be in the proportion of twenty-four feet long to fourteen wide. The Union to be one-third the length of the flag and as deep as the upper seven stripes.

On September 18, 1818, the Navy Department ordered a change in the order of arranging the stars

```
*   *   *   *   *
*   *   *   *   *
*   *   *   *   *
*   *   *   *   *
```
in the Union, so that they should conform to this second diagram.

The Naval Standard Ensign is now a flag thirty-six feet long and nineteen feet hoist; with a union fourteen feet, four and eight-tenths inches long, and extending from the top of the flag to the lower edge of the seventh stripe; the stars in the union are arranged in six rows—two of eight and four of seven stars each.

Besides this Standard Ensign, the Navy Regulations describe about fifty variations—ranging from one seventy feet long and six inches wide, to another which is five feet long and two feet six inches hoist.

ARMY FLAGS.

THE GARRISON FLAG, is the Official National Flag, and the one used generally for all display and celebration purposes outside of the Navy and shipping. The Garrison Flag is of bunting, thirty-six feet long and twenty feet hoist, made up of thirteen equally wide alternate Red and White stripes, beginning and ending with the Red. The Union, in the upper quarter next to the staff, is one-third the length of the flag, and extends to the lower edge of the seventh stripe, counting from the top. It contains as many white five-pointed stars as there are States in the Union, now forty-four. (See note, page 8.)

The Army Regulations, like those of the Navy,

describe quite a number of smaller official flags—one as small as two feet five inches fly, by two feet three inches on the staff.

The Stars and Stripes were first displayed in what is now California, in the fall of 1829. James P. Arther, a Hollander, and a citizen of Massachusetts, was mate of a trading vessel. He and a party of men were ashore at San Diego, curing hides. They made a flag with which to attract and salute the vessels that occasionally passed within sight of their camp. This flag was manufactured from the shirts of the party. This was, of course, long before there was any thought of that region ever becoming a part of the United States.

In the early summer of 1846, "a baker's dozen" of Americans determined to take possession of the Pacific Coast in the name of the United States. They constructed a flag from the white cotton and red flannel underclothes of an old lady, who generously, for this purpose, reduced her already scanty wardrobe. On this flag they painted a bear—with such artistic success that the Spaniards mistook it for a hog. This "Hog Flag" was raised at Sonoma, on June 14, 1846, and it is still preserved as a precious memento by the Pioneer Society of San Francisco.

On July 4th, of the same year, General John C. Fremont presided over a meeting of the Americans of Sonoma, at which it was declared that the country thereabout belonged to the United States. War was also declared against Mexico to establish this pronunciamento. Fremont and his associates were entirely ignorant of the war then actually going on with Mexico.

The flag over Fremont's headquarters had only one star in the Union. Whether this was the indication that California was—like Texas—an independent nation or not, has never been fully determined, although that seems to have been the idea of some of those engaged in that enterprise.

Commodore Sloat, of the Savannah, raised the Stars and Stripes at Monterey, July 7, 1846; and Captain Montgomery, of the Portsmouth, hoisted the American Standard at Yerba Buena, now San Francisco, on the following day.

Lieutenant Lynch, in 1848, carried the American Flag over Palestine, making it a point to display the Stars and Stripes at all the principal points and on all important occasions.

Lieutenant Stone, on April 11, 1848, planted the American Standard upon the extreme summit of Mount Popocatepetl, Mexico.

Dr. Hayes, on May 18, 1861, hoisted the Stars and Stripes in latitude 81°25′ North, longitude 70°30′ West—the most northerly point ever reached by civilized man, on land.

Lieutenant Frederick Schwatka, of the United States Army, unfurled the Stars and Stripes at the North Magnetic Pole, on July 4, 1879.

When Texas came into the Union on December

29, 1845, her National Flag was—as it had been adopted January 25, 1839—a blue perpendicular stripe next to the staff, occupying one-third of the entire flag. In this was a central, single, white, five-pointed star, one point up. The balance of the flag was of two equal horizontal stripes, the upper one White, the lower one Red. The Naval flag, previously adopted, was the same as the United States Standard, except that there was only one star in the Union.

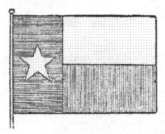

TEXAS FLAG.

The first hostile act in the drama of secession occurred on January 10, 1861, when the steamer, Star of the West, laden with provisions for the garrison at Fort Sumter and carrying the Stars and Stripes was fired upon by the South Carolina forces as she was entering Charleston harbor.

The first regular attack upon the National property, authority and Flag was in the firing upon Fort Sumter on the morning of April 12, 1861. Major Robert Anderson with a very small support defended the position most gallantly and stubbornly, and capitulated to overpowering numbers upon terms which allowed him and his heroic men to carry with them their private property and arms, as well as to salute their Flag, lower it themselves and carry it away with them. The Stars and Stripes were again raised over the retaken ruins of Fort Sumter on February 18, 1865.

The attack on Fort Sumter and the forced lowering of the National Standard there, was the signal for raising millions of flags all over the now aroused country.

In the Seceding States there was a great variety of banners—the blue flag, the various State flags, the special colors of different military companies and civic organizations, as well as many old time and newly invented designs.

In the Loyal States the spontaneous and burning indignation over the cutting insult offered to the Flag, mingled with equally burning enthusiasm of all classes in favor of the grand principles of liberty and union—past, present and perpetual—found impulsive, immediate and universal expression in raising or displaying everywhere the Stars and Stripes. The venerable patriarch and the toddling child, the gray-haired grandmother and the sunny-haired boy, the earnest matron and the modest maiden, the determined man of mature years and the impulsive youth, the millionaire capitalist and the humblest wage-worker, the peace-preaching clergyman and the tactics-drilling militiaman, the native born American and the naturalized citizen, all were one in sentiment, all were one in desire, all were one in impulsive and immediate action. Everyone reverenced the Flag—its memories, its meanings and its glories—everyone raised or waved or wore the Flag;

everyone cheered or saluted the Flag. The Flags
displayed were of all sizes—large, medium and tiny;
they were of all kinds of material—silk, woolen,
linen, cotton or mixed—and even of paper; they
were of every possible grade of texture—coarse, fine
and gossamer; they were of all modes of manufacture—woven, dyed, painted and patch-work; their
cost was measured by eagles, by dollars, by dimes,
by cents, and by even fractions of a cent; they
were paid for in gold, silver, copper and promises.
These Flags were raised upon public buildings and
private residences, upon church steeples and store
fronts, upon liberty poles and walking canes, upon
mast-heads, yard-arms and coach-whips.   These
Flags were worn by men on their hats or in their
button-holes, and they adorned the bonnets and the
bosoms of women.

In all this seemingly chaotic diversity there was,
however, a conspicuous and unbroken uniformity.
These innumerable millions of Flags, which in these
April days came forth as if by magic, blossoming in
the warm spring sun of aroused patriotism, were all
made of the same colors, in the same order and
proportion, and fashioned after the same design.
Every one of these countless Flags, by whomsoever
displayed, every one of them—wherever seen, every
one of them—of whatever size, material or texture,
everyone of them was " Red, White and Blue;"
everyone of them was the Stars and Stripes; everyone of them was the unique, the recognized and the

glorious Standard of the United States—the Flag of
" Liberty and Union." Everywhere the Old Flag of
past days and of glorious memories was raised aloft
until it waved in the breeze, unfurling its clear colors in the radiant sun, as the present emblem of that
living enthusiasm which declares that this glorious
Union, as the result and bulwark of man's freedom,
" must and shall be preserved." The prose of its
past history was at once transformed into the living
poetry of its present grandeur.   The respect for its
past sentiment, and the esteem for its past supporters, was instantly aroused into the now living meaning, and into the now vital enthusiasm, which pledged
fortune and life to maintain and perpetuate the
union and the liberty, the purity and the national
integrity, which this Standard represents.

The one sentiment and song was as if the whole
populace had joined in one acclaim:

"Oh raise the glorious Ensign high
    And let the nations see
The Flag for which our fathers fought
    To make our country free."

O, raise on high the Stars and Stripes
    And let all peoples see
That we will live—or we will die—
    To keep our country free.

Edward Everett, in a most finished and enthusiastic address, struck the key-note of those days when
at a flag meeting, in Boston, he said :

" Why is it that the Flag of the Country, always honored, always beloved, is now at once worshiped. I may say, with the passionate homage of the whole people ? Why does it float, as never before, not only from arsenal and mast-head, but from tower and steeple, from public edifices, the temples of science. the private dwellings, in magnificent display of miniature representation ? Let Fort Sumter give the answer. *   *   * "

THE CONFEDERATE FLAG.

"The Flag of the Confederate States of America shall consist of a red field, with a white space extending horizontally through the center, and equal in width to one-third the width of the flag; the red spaces above and below to be of the same width as the white. The union blue, extending down through the white space, and stopping at the lower red space ; in the center of the union a circle of white stars, corresponding in number with the States of the Confederacy."

Adopted March 5, 1861, but entered upon the journal of proceedings as of the day previous, when it had been first publicly displayed over the State House at Montgomery, Alabama, where the Provisional Confederate Congress was then in session.

The " Stars and Bars " was not generally used by the secession army, the usual battle-flag being one with a red field, having a blue diagonal cross containing white stars.

The second Confederate Flag, adopted in May, 1863, was as follows:

"The field was of white, twice as long as wide. The union was red, square and two-thirds as deep as the field, with a broad, white-bordered saltier, emblazoned with five-pointed white stars, corresponding in number to the States in the Confederacy."

This was superseded, on February 14, 1865, by the following flag :

"Width, two-thirds of its length; the union three-fifths of the width of the flag, and so proportioned as to leave the length of field on the side of the union twice the width below it ; to have a ground of red, and broad blue saltier thereon, bordered with white, and emblazoned with mullets, or five-pointed stars, corresponding in number to that of the Confederate States. The field to be white, except the outer half from the union, which shall be a red bar extending the width of the flag."

The Stars and Stripes were again raised over the surrendered Confederate Capitol at Richmond, Va., on April 3, 1865, by Lieutenant Johnston L. de Peyster, assisted by Captain Langdon.

General U. S. Grant, commanding the Union armies, received the complete and final formal surrender of the Confederate Forces, from their Commanding General, R. E. Lee, on April 9, 1865. It is a notable coincidence, that many interpret as a glorious harbinger of great good, that this date was upon Sunday, and Palm Sunday at that; and that thus peace was finally restored to the nation on the anniversary of the day when the Prince of Peace, as the multitudes with loud hosannas strewed mantles, flowers and palm branches in his path, made his glorious and regal, entry into the Holy City—Jerusalem —"the City of Jehovah's Peace."

Major Robert Anderson evacuated Fort Sumter on April 14, 1861. On the fourth anniversary of that date, April 14, 1865, when he was Major-General Anderson, he had the proud satisfaction and the distinguished honor of again raising over the dismantled ruins of that fortress the same battle-begrimed flag which he had so gallantly defended when he was, four years before, overpowered. This ceremony was accompanied by a salute of one hundred guns from the now retaken fort, by a national salute from every fort and battery that had fired upon the positions, by a grand display of bunting from shipping and soldiery, and amid the glad acclaim and huzzas of Navy, Army and civilians present, the whole winding up with a grand collation and a characteristic address from Henry Ward Beecher.

It is not within the scope of this little book to attempt even an outline history of the late Civil War. It is, however, appropriate in this connection to record that the Stars and Stripes led an army and received the support of a people who, for courageous patriotism and earnest philanthropy, have no precedent in history. From the President in his chair—than whom none has proved more worthy, to the humblest wage-worker in his shop, and from the Commanding General of the Armies — whose memory we all delight to honor, to the humblest musketeer or drummer boy in the ranks, only one sentiment prevailed, and only one mandate found any indorsement: "THE UNION MUST AND SHALL BE PRESERVED." And this zealous sentiment of love for the " Red, White and Blue," when woven into the Stars and Stripes, and thus forming Our Flag, which symbolizes our nation and our ideal of its ideal development toward perfection, and this hearty and intelligent recognition of its patriotic and philanthropic supporters and defenders, was not only enthusiastic and exalted, but it is universal and permanent as well.

We have the memoirs and the monuments of Washington and Franklin, of Roger Williams and William Penn, of Patrick Henry and Daniel Webster, of Lincoln and Grant ; and we have the green—and frequently unmarked—and even unknown graves of the unnumbered and patriotic hosts, who sustained and followed the lead of these illustrious men. These mighty and unhistoried hosts, whose names are seldom or never pronounced, it should be remembered, formed the armies that shed blood and gave up life " in the defense of Our Flag and the Right," and thus gave these recognized leaders of the nation their place among the good and great men of the earth. And now, year by year, as our " Decoration

Day" annually recurs, the Stars and Stripes wave alike bright, glorious and eulogistic over the grandest monument of the most illustrious statesman, and over the modest headstone of the humblest soldier; and the heaven-distilled incense of fragrant and beautiful flowers rises alike sweet and worshipful from the stately tomb of the greatest general, and from the unmarked grave of the patriotic, but now unknown, volunteer.

LINCOLN AND EMANCIPATION.

Lincoln emancipated the slaves held to servitude in the United States; and this action on his part, and its acceptance by the people and its ratification by Congress, is certainly very intimately connected with the preservation of the Union.

It is usually said that Lincoln sacrificed slavery as an important factor in saving the Union, and thus perpetuating the life and the integrity of the Nation. The grand truth, however, is that the Union was saved that slavery might die.

The great struggle of the late Civil War was inaugurated, primarily, with the single purpose of perpetuating and extending slavery on the Western Continent. The attempted secession of the revolting States was only one step, and the formation of the Confederacy was simply another step, towards the one end of making slavery a perpetual—or at least a more permanent—as well as a more extended institution. Had secession succeeded, and the

Confederacy thus become an independent government, human bondage and chattelism in man—the
doctrine that the slave has no rights which the master
is bound to respect—would have seemingly become
not "a relic of barbarism," but a recognized and
representative feature of American Civilization. The
Union, like the Declaration of Independence, was
based upon the eternal principle of the equal rights
of man as an individual; and the Union has been
preserved, and always will be preserved, upon this
unchangeable foundation. The Union was preserved in the late Civil War, because, by its integrity
and continuance, human slavery was branded as
barbarous and inhuman, and also doomed to immediate abolition.

What Lincoln meant or intended in issuing the
Emancipation Proclamation, or why the people
endorsed it, or why Congress ratified it, is of comparatively little importance now; for the recognized
grand truth is: the Union was formed upon, and the
Stars and Stripes symbolize, a principle grander than
even the Union—the equal rights of man as man.
The principle founding the Union saved the Union,
and saving the Union perfects what founding the
Union inaugurated, and what **Our Glorious Flag**
represents—FREEDOM.

CHAPTER IV.

SELECTIONS ELOQUENT, PATRIOTIC AND POETICAL.

LIBERTY AND UNION, NOW AND FOREVER, ONE AND INSEPARABLE.

"When my eyes shall turn to behold, for the last time, the sun in heaven, may I not see him shining on the broken and dishonored fragments of a once glorious Union; on States dissevered, discordant, belligerent; on a land rent with civil feuds, or drenched, it may be, in fraternal blood. Let their last feeble and lingering glance rather behold the gorgeous ensign of the Republic, now known and honored throughout the earth, still full high advanced, its arms and trophies streaming in their original lustre, not a stripe erased or polluted, not a single star obscured, bearing for its motto no such miserable interrogatory as, *What is all this worth?* nor those other words of delusion and folly, *Liberty first and Union afterwards*; but everywhere spread all over in characters of living light, blazing in all its ample folds as they float over the sea and

over the land, and in every wind under the whole
heaven, that other sentiment, dear to every true
American heart, 'Liberty and Union, now and forever, one and inseparable.' "—WEBSTER.

ONE COUNTRY, CONSTITUTION AND DESTINY.

" We will swear anew, and teach the oath to
our children, that, with God's help, the American
Republic shall stand unmoved, though all the
powers of piracy and European jealousy should
combine to overthrow it; that we shall have in the
future, as we have in the past, *one country, one constitution, one destiny;* and that when we shall have
passed from earth, and the acts of to-day shall be matters of history, and the dark power which sought our
overthrow shall have been overthrown, our sons may
gather strength from our example in every contest
with despotism that time may have in store to try
their virtue, and that they may rally under the
Stars and Stripes with our olden war cry, " Liberty
and Union, now and forever, one and inseparable."
—JOHN JAY.

SYMBOLISM.

" It is in and through symbols that man con-
sciously or unconsciously lives, moves, and has his
being. Those ages, moreover, are accounted the
noblest which can best recognize symbolic worth
and prize it at the highest."—CARLYLE.

"As at the early dawn the stars shine forth, even while it grows light, and then, as the sun advances, that light breaks into banks and streaming lines of color, the glowing red and the intense white striving together and ribbing the horizon with bars effulgent, so on the American Flag—stars and beams of many-colored light shine out together. And where this Flag comes, and men behold it, they see in its sacred emblazonry no ramping lions, no fierce eagle, no embattled castles or insignia of imperial authority. They see the symbol of light. It is the banner of dawn. It means *Liberty;* and the galley slave, the poor, oppressed conscript, the down-trodden creature of foreign despotism, sees in the American Flag that very promise and prediction of God: 'The people which sat in darkness saw a great light, and to them which sat in the region and shadow of death light is sprung up.'

" In 1777, within a few days of one year after the Declaration of Independence, the Congress of the Colonies in the Confederated States assembled and ordained this glorious National Flag which we now hold and defend, and advanced its full light before God and all men as the Flag of Liberty.

" It was no holiday flag gorgeously emblazoned for gayety or vanity. It was a solemn National Signal. When that banner first unrolled to the sun, it was the symbol of all those holy truths and purposes which brought together the Colonial American Congress! Our Flag **carries** American ideas,

American history and American feelings. Beginning
with the Colonies and coming down to our time,
in its sacred heraldry, in its glorious insignia, it has
gathered and stored chiefly this supreme idea : *Divine
right of Liberty in Man*. Every color means Liberty ; every thread means Liberty ; every form of
star and beam or stripe of light means Liberty—not
lawlessness, not license; but organized, institutional
Liberty—Liberty through law, and laws for Liberty.

"It is not a painted rag. It is a whole National
history. It is the Constitution. It is the Government. It is the free people that stand in the Government on the Constitution."—HENRY WARD BEECHER.

DUTY TO OUR FLAG.

"When the Standard of the Union is raised and
waves over my head, the Standard which Washington
planted on the ramparts of the constitution, God for-
bid that I should inquire whom the people have com-
missioned to unfurl it and bear it up. I only ask in
what manner, as an humble individual, I can best discharge my duties defending it."—DANIEL WEBSTER.

THE FLAG RULES.

"Every man must be for the United States or
against it. * * * It is the duty of every American citizen to rally round the Flag of his Country."
—STEPHEN A. DOUGLAS.

Dr. Lyman Abbott, in a recent address, used substantially the following language, which is surely worth preservation and frequent reading :

"If the Kingdom of Heaven is anything but a mocking mirage, it must consist in and come forth in the form of the Universal Brotherhood of Man.

"Social reform in the strict line of natural evolution can come to pass only under two conditions: First, the supreme duty of society is toward the moral education of individuals ; second, the supreme duty of individuals is toward the moral education of society. Society, as a whole, creates its individuals, and moral education completes the creative work. The family, a natural institution founded on the distinction of sex, is the fundamental social institution, and ought to be the fundamental moral institution. Society is nothing but what its own members make it. Each individual counts for one in determining the moral quality of social action, and the duty he owes to society culminates in making society moral through his own personal effort. The reciprocal duty as between society and individuals rests upon their relations one to the other. Our social perplexities are all the result of disregard of the fundamental laws of our social body. We are all moral beings simply because we are, in the first place, organic beings. To live for self alone is pure selfishness. To live for others alone would be pure selfishness. The only moral life would be to live for both in even balance between altruism and egoism. It is only this equilibrium that renders possible a social system. How to secure universal moral education is the most pressing, practical problem of our time. What more can society do for the individual than to make him? What greater wrong can society do than to leave him half made? The child is born into the right to be taught how to live."

The "Stars and Stripes" will forever symbolize this transcendent and ideal principle; and the Flag of our Nation continually announces that this beautiful ideal of philanthropy and intelligence is becoming, in the individual American citizen—and hence in the American people—more and more the realized attainment.

MEANING OF OUR FLAG.

Alfred B. Street speaks of the Flag in the following glowing terms:

"The stars of the new flag represent a constellation of States rising in the west. The idea was taken from the constellation Lyra, which, in the hands of Orpheus, signified harmony. The blue of the field was taken from the edges of the Covenanter's banner in Scotland, significant also of the league and covenant of the united Colonies against oppression, and involving the virtues of vigilance, perseverance, and justice. The stars were disposed in a circle, symbolizing the perpetuity of the Union, the ring like serpent of the Egyptians signifying eternity. The thirteen stripes showed, with the stars, the number of the united Colonies, and denotes the subordination of the States to the Union, as well as equality among themselves. The whole was a blending of the various flags previous to the Union Flag—the red flag of the army and the white one of-the floating batteries. The red color, which, in Roman days, was the signal of defiance, denotes daring, while the white suggests purity. What eloquence do the stars breathe when their full significance is known! a new constellation, union, perpetuity, a covenant against oppression; justice, equality, subordination, courage and purity."

MYSTIC MEANING OF OUR FLAG.

"There is the National Flag! He must be cold indeed, who can look upon its folds rippling in the breeze without pride of country. If he be in a foreign land the Flag is companionship, and country itself, with all its endearments. Who, as he sees it, can think of a State merely? Whose eye, once fastened upon its radiant trophies can fail to recognize the image of the whole nation? It has been called "a floating piece of poetry," and yet 1 know not if it have any intrinsic beauty beyond other ensigns. Its highest beauty is what it symbolizes. It is because it represents all, that all gaze at it with delight and reverence. It is a piece of bunting lifted in the air, but it speaks sublimely, and every part has a voice. Its Stripes of alternate Red and White proclaim the original *union* of thirteen States to maintain the Declaration of Independence. Its Stars, White on a field of Blue, proclaim that *union* of States constituting our national constellation, which receives a new star with every new State. The two, together, signify *union*, past and present. The very colors have a language which was officially recognized by our fathers. White is for purity, Red for valor, Blue for justice, and, altogether,—bunting, stripes, stars and colors blazing in the sky,—make the Flag of Our Country to be cherished by all our hearts, to be upheld by all our hands.—CHARLES SUMNER.

SYMBOLISM OF OUR FLAG.

The United States Government is the only one in the world based upon the fundamental principle of the absolute equal rights of every citizen; that the Government is the machinery and servant of the citizen; and that the citizen determines the rights and powers of the Government.

The three departments of the Government—the legislative, judicial and executive—are coördinate as they should be; for the will, the intellect, and procedure—to which they correspond, and which they therefore represent—are coördinate.

The National Flag is also in perfect harmony with the above ideas; for the red represents love, will, aspiration; the white stands for wisdom, intellect, and plan; these are appropriately arranged in stripes which are narrow and alternating, to type their intimate and constant relationship and coördinate operation ; the red, or will, is the first or lower stripe to show that on the will is based all else; the red is the last or topmost stripe to announce that all will and all intelligence is for the sake of the highest and purest inspiration ; the white is striped between to teach the constant necessity of intelligence in all operations of good.

The blue, which represents operation or activity, is massed in the upper corner. The full length stripes of red and white below this blue field teach that purity and intelligence is the foundation of, and, therefore, should precede the mere effort to achieve great things. The stripes which are on the same level as the blue field—of active effort, symbolize the truth that purity and intelligence should be the constant incentive and guide of every act. The stars represent not only the individual States, but also type the individual citizen, in all his rights, duties, and aspirations. They also show that the grand and full field of operation—represented by the blue—is only a field of potential possibilities, which, like an unlit and solidly azure sky, has neither use, beauty, or even recognition, until lighted and adorned by the glorious stars of special and definite results, which shine out in their varying size of pure aspiration, in the differing brilliancy of intelligent plan, and in the graded grandeur of the good accomplished.

So Our Glorious Flag, as it waves on high, will
type to all the red radiance of the purest philanthropic aspirations ; the white, clearness of the illu-
minated intellect; and the practical blue, procedure
of active power; with the glorious stars of grand
attainments. —LLEBNELTRE.

THE VOICE OF OUR FLAG.

" The National ensign, pure and simple, dearer to
our hearts at this moment, as we lift it to the gale
and see no other sign of hope upon the storm-cloud
which rolls and settles above it, save that which is
reflected from its own radiant hues.   Dearer, a thou-
sand-fold dearer, to us all than ever it was before,
while gilded by the sunshine of our prosperity, and
playing with the zephyrs of peace.   It speaks for
itself far more eloquently than I can speak for it.
Behold it !   Listen to it !   Every star has a tongue.
Every stripe is articulate.   There is no language or
speech where their voices are not heard.   There is
magic in the web of it.   It has an answer for every
question.   It has a solution for every doubt and every
perplexity.   It has a word of good cheer for every
hour of gloom or despondency.   Behold it !   Listen
to it !   It speaks of earlier and later struggles.   It
speaks of heroes and patriots among the living and
among the dead.   But before all and above all other
associations and memories, whether of glorious men

or of glorious deeds, or glorious places, its voice is ever of union and liberty, of the constitution and the laws. Behold it! Listen to it! Let it tell the story of its birth to these gallant volunteers as they march beneath its folds by day, or repose beneath its sentinel stars by night. Let it recall to them the strange, eventful history of its rise and progress. Let it rehearse to them the wondrous tale of its trials and its triumphs in peace as well as in war."—ROBERT C. WINTHROP.

THE BEAUTIFUL FLAG.

"I have seen the glories of art and architecture, and of mountain and river. I have seen the sun set on Jungfrau and the full moon rise over Mount Blanc, but the fairest vision on which these eyes ever looked was the Flag of my own country in a foreign land. Beautiful as a flower to those who love it, terrible as a meteor to those who hate it, it is the symbol of the power and the glory and the honor of fifty millions of Americans."—GEO. F. HOAR.

FRATERNITY.

"I trust the time is not far distant when, under the crossed swords and the locked shields of Americans, North and South, our people shall sleep in peace and rise in liberty, love and harmony, under the union of Our Flag—the Stars and Stripes."—GARFIELD.

THE FLAG OF OUR UNION.

BY GEORGE P. MORRIS.

A song for our banner, the watchword recall,
　Which gave the republic her station—
" United we stand, divided we fall! "
　It made and preserves us a nation.

The union of lakes, the union of lands,
　The union of States none can sever!
The union of hearts, the union of hands,
　And the Flag of our Union forever and ever,
　The Flag of our Union forever.

What God in His infinite wisdom designed,
　And armed with republican thunder;
Not all the earth's despots and factions combined
　Have the power to conquer or sunder.
　　The union of lakes, etc.

Oh! keep that flag flying! The pride of the van!
　To all other nations display it.
The ladies for union are all to a—man!
　And not to the man who'd betray it.
　　The union of lakes, etc.

THE FLAG AND THE LAW.

" There are two things holy—the flag which represents military honor, and the law which represents
the national right."—VICTOR HUGO.

YANKEE DOODLE.

Yankee Doodle is a musical favorite of very uncertain age, cosmopolitan nationality and unknown authorship. With slight local variations it has been played, and with appropriate local versions it has been sung, in nearly all the countries of Europe, so long that the memory of the oldest inhabitants received it as a traditional favorite from their ancestors. The different sentiments expressed by it and the various rhymes adapted to it are simply innumerable. One of the many jingles adapted to it in Colonial times very well describes it thus:

Yankee Doodle is the tune
    Americans delight in,
'Twill do to whistle, sing or play,
    And it is just the thing for fighting.

The most popular version in word, and one commonly used in revolutionary times, and said to have been sung at the battle of Bunker Hill, is the following:

Father and I went down to camp,
    Along with Captain Gooding,
And there we saw the men and boys,
    As thick as hasty pudding.

Yankee Doodle, keep it up,
    Yankee Doodle dandy!
Mind the music and the step,
    And with the girls be handy!

And there we see a thousand men,
  As rich as 'Squire David,
And what they wasted every day,—
  I wish it had been saved.
    Yankee Doodle, etc.

The 'lasses they used every day,
  Would keep our house all winter,—
They have so much, that I'll be bound,
  They eat when they've a mind to.
    Yankee Doodle, etc.

And there we saw a whoppin' gun,
  As big as a log of maple,
Mounted on a little cart,—
  A load for father's cattle.
    Yankee Doodle, etc.

And every time they fired it off
  It took a horn of powder,
And made a noise like father's gun,
  Only a nation louder.
    Yankee Doodle, etc.

I went as near unto it
  As 'Siah's underpinning;
Father went as nigh agin,—
  I thought the devil was in him.
    Yankee Doodle, etc.

Cousin Simon grew so bold,
  I thought he meant to cock it;

He scared me so, I streaked it off
  And hung to father's pocket.
      Yankee Doodle, etc.

And Captain Davis had a gun
  He kind o' clapped his hand on,
And struck a crooked stabbing-iron
  Upon the little end on't.
      Yankee Doodle, etc.

And there I saw a pumpkin shell
  As big as mother's basin;
And every time they sent one off,
  They scampered like tarnation.
      Yankee Doodle, etc.

I saw a little barrel, too,
  It's heads were made of leather;
They knocked on it with little clubs,
  To call the men together.
      Yankee Doodle, etc.

And there was Captain Washington,
  With grand folks all about him;
They say he's grown so tarnal proud,
  He cannot ride without them.
      Yankee Doodle, etc.

He had on his meeting-clothes,
  And rode a strapping stallion;
And gave his orders to his men—
  I guess there was a million.
      Yankee Doodle, etc.

And then the feathers in his hat,
   They were so tarnal fine-ah,
I wanted peskily to get
   To hand to my Jemima.
      Yankee Doodle, etc.

And then they'd fife away like fun.
   And play on cornstalk fiddles;
And some had ribbons red as blood
   All wound around their middles.
      Yankee Doodle, etc.

The troopers, too, would gallop up,
   And fire right in our faces.
It scared me a' most to death,
   To see them run such races.
      Yankee Doodle, etc.

And then I saw a snarl of men
   A-digging graves, they told me,
So tarnal long, so tarnal deep—
   They allowed they were to hold me.
      Yankee Doodle, etc.

It scared me so I hoofed it off,
   Nor stopped, as I remember,
Nor turned about, till I got home,
   Locked up in mother's chamber.
      Yankee Doodle, etc.

THE AMERICAN FLAG.

BY JOSEPH RODMAN DRAKE.

The American Flag was written when the author was in his twenty-fourth year, and first published, a few days after its completion, in the New York Evenn,g *Post* on May 29, 1819. Fitz Greene Halleck is the author of the last four lines as the poem is now published.

When Freedom from her mountain height
　Unfurled her standard to the air,
She tore the azure robe of night,
　And set the stars of glory there.
She mingled with its gorgeous dyes
The milky baldrick of the skies,
And striped its pure celestial white
With streakings of the morning light;
Then from his mansion in the sun
She called her eagle-bearer down,
And gave into his mighty hand
The symbol of her chosen land.

Majestic monarch of the cloud!
　Who rear'st aloft thy eagle form
To hear the tempest trumping loud,
　And see the lightning lances driven,
　When strides the warrior of the storm,
　And rolls the thunder-drum of heaven!
Child of the Sun! to thee 'tis given
　To guard the banner of the free!

To hover in the sulphur smoke,
To ward away the battle stroke,
And bid its blending shine afar,
Like rainbows on the cloud of war,
  The harbingers of victory.

Flag of the brave! thy folds shall fly,
The sign of hope and triumph high;
When speaks the trumpet's signal tone,
And the long line comes gleaming on,
Ere yet the life-blood warm and wet,
Has dimmed the glistening bayonet,
Each soldier's eye shall brightly turn
To where thy sky-born glories burn;
And, as his springy steps advance,
Catch war and vengeance from the glance;
And when thy cannon mouthings loud
Heave in wild weather the battle shroud,
And gory sabers rise and fall
Like shooting flames on midnight pall,
Then shall thy meteor glances glow,
  And cowering foes shall sink beneath
Each gallant arm that strikes below
  That lovely messenger of death!

Flag of the seas! on Ocean's wave
Thy stars shall glitter o'er the brave;
When death, careering on the gale,
Sweeps darkly round the bellied sail,
And frighted waves rush wildly back
Before the broadsides reeling rack,

Each dying wanderer at sea
Shall look at once to Heaven and thee,
And smile to see thy splendors fly
In triumph o'er his closing eye.

Flag of the free heart's hope and home
    By angels' hands to valor given;
Thy stars have lit the welkin dome,
    And all thy hues are born in Heaven.
Forever float that standard sheet!
    Where breathes the foe but falls before us,
With Freedom's soil beneath our feet
    And Freedom's banner streaming o'er us.

THE STAR-SPANGLED BANNER.

BY FRANCIS SCOTT KEY.

TUNE.—*Anacreon in Heaven.*

The Star-Spangled Banner was composed during the night between September 13 and 14, 1814. Francis Scott Key, of Georgetown, left Baltimore in a vessel bearing a flag of truce, for the purpose of securing the release of a friend who was held by the British forces as a prisoner of war. He was held at the mouth of the Patapsco, because his return might disclose an intended attack upon Baltimore. During the day of the 13th he witnessed the bombardment of Fort McHenry, and into the darkness of the night. Then in the darkness he watched the bombshells as they shot through the air, listening anxiously to their explosions. After the firing ceased,

he waited, in painful suspense, for the first dawning
of the morning twilight, anxious to know whether
the fort had fallen or the enemy withdrawn—which
would be indicated by the flag—the English Union
or the Stars and Stripes—which should be flying over
the position.   His glass was almost constantly in use
until, as the light became clearer, he finally saw that
"Our Flag was still there." Chief Justice Taney, his
brother-in-law, says, "The scene which he describes,
and the warm spirit of patriotism which breathes
in the song, were not the offspring of mere fancy or
poetic imagination. He describes what he actually
saw, and he tells us what he felt while witnessing the
conflict, and what he felt when the battle was over
and the victory won by his countrymen.   Every
word came warm from his heart, and for that reason,
even more than its poetical merit, it never fails to
find response in the hearts of those who listen to it."
It was originally called

"THE DEFENSE OF FORT M'HENRY;"

and this is the heading given it when first printed on
slips and published in the *Baltimore American*.

Oh! say, can you see by the dawn's early light
  What so proudly we hailed at the twilight's last
      gleaming,
Whose broad stripes and bright stars through the
      perilous fight,
  O'er the ramparts we watched, were so gallantry
      streaming?

And the rocket's red glare,
The bombs bursting in air,
Gave proof through the night that our flag was
    still there.
  Oh! say, does the star-spangle banner yet wave
  O'er the land of the free and the home of the
      brave?

On the shore, dimly seen through the mists of the
      deep,
  Where the foe's haughty host in dread silence
      reposes,
What is that which the breeze, o'er the towering
      steep,
  As it fitfully blows, half conceals, half discloses?
Now it catches the gleam
Of the morning's first beam,
In full glory reflected now shines on the stream.
  'Tis the star-spangled banner; oh! long may it wave
  O'er the land of the free and the home of the brave.

And where is the foe that so vauntingly swore
  Mid the havoc of war and the battle's confusion,
A home and a country they'd leave us no more?
  Their blood has washed out their foul footsteps'
      pollution.
No refuge could save
The hireling and slave
From the terror of flight or the gloom of the grave;
  And the star-spangle banner in triumph doth wave
  O'er the land of the free and the home of the brave.

Oh! thus be it ever when freemen shall stand
  Between their loved homes and war's desolation;
Blest with victory and peace, may the Heav'n-rescued
      land
  Praise the Power that hath made and preserved
      us a nation!
Then conquer we must,
When our cause it is just,
And this be our motto,—"In God is our trust;"
  And the star-spangled banner in triumph shall
      wave
O'er the land of the free and the home of the brave.

The Star-Spangled Banner has been printed,
recited and sung with many variations from its orig-
nal form. There has also been frequent substitutions
of lines and stanzas, with not a few additions, to
serve a temporary or local necessity.

HAIL COLUMBIA.

BY JOSEPH HOPKINSON.

TUNE—*The President's March.*

Hail Columbia—happy land,
Hail ye heroes—heaven-born band,
Who fought and bled in Freedom's cause,
Who fought and bled in Freedom's cause,
And when the storm of war was done,
Enjoyed the peace your valor won—

Let Independence be our boast,
Ever mindful what it cost;
Ever grateful for the prize,
Let its altars reach the skies.
  Firm united let us be,
  Rallying round our liberty,
  As a band of brothers joined ;
  Peace and safety we shall find.

Immortal Patriots, rise once more,
Defend your rights, defend your shore;
Let no rude foe with impious hand,
Let no rude foe with impious hand,
Invade the shrine, where sacred lies,
Of toil and blood, the well-earned prize.
  While offering Peace, sincere and just,
  In Heaven we place a manly trust,
  That Truth and Justice will prevail,
  And every scheme of bondage fail.
    Firm, united, let us be,
    Rallying round our Liberty,
    As a band of brothers joined,
    Peace and safety we shall find.

Sound, sound the trump of fame,
Let WASHINGTON's great name
Ring through the world with loud applause,
Ring through the world with loud applause.
Let every clime to Freedom dear,
Listen with a joyful ear;
  With equal skill, with godlike power,
  He governs in the fearful hour

Of horrid war; or guides with ease
The happier times of honest peace.
  Firm, united, let us be,
  Rallying round our Liberty,
  As a band of brothers joined;
  Peace and safety we shall find.

Behold the chief, who now commands,
Once more to serve his country stands,
The rock on which the storm will beat,
The rock on which the storm will beat,
But arm'd in virtue, firm and true,
His hopes are fixed on Heaven and you.
  When hope was sinking in dismay,
  And clouds obscured Columbia's day,
  His steady mind, from changes free,
  Resolved on *Death or Liberty*.
  Firm, united, let us be,
  Rallying round our Liberty,
  As a band of brothers joined;
  Peace and safety we shall find

NOTHING BUT FLAGS.

BY MOSES OWEN.

A party of sight seers were "doing" the State
Capitol, at Augusta, Maine. Coming to the elegant
case in the rotunda in which are arranged the Colors
which her regiments carried so gallantly during the
late civil war, they passed it by with a cursory look

—one of the number remarking—"All that nice case for nothing but flags." That remark inspired the following poem; and thus does unappreciative stolidity often arouse genius and make it eloquent:

"NOTHING BUT FLAGS!" but simple flags,
Tattered and torn, and hanging in rags;
And we walk beneath them with careless tread
Nor think of the hosts of the mighty dead
Who have marched beneath them in days gone by,
With a burning cheek and a kindling eye,
And have bathed their folds with the young life's tide,
And dying, blessed them, and blessing died.

"NOTHING BUT FLAGS!" yet methinks at night
They tell each other their tales of fright!
And dim spectres come, and their thin arms twine
Round each standard torn, as they stand in line.
As the word is given—they change! they form!
And the dim hall rings with the battle's storm!
And once again, through the smoke and strife,
Those colors lead to a Nation's life.

"NOTHING BUT FLAGS!" yet they're bathed with tears,
They tell of triumphs, of hopes, of fears;
Of a mother's prayers, of a boy away,
Of a serpent crushed, of a coming day.
Silent they speak, and the tear *will* start,
As we stand beneath them with throbbing heart,
And think of those who are never forgot—
Their flags come home—why come *they* not?

"NOTHING BUT FLAGS!" yet we hold our breath,
And gaze with awe at these types of death!
"Nothing but flags!" yet the thought will come,
The heart must pray, though the lips be dumb.
They are sacred, pure, and we see no stain
On those dear-loved flags come home again;
Baptized in blood, our purest, best,
Tattered and torn, they're now at rest.

AMERICA.

BY SAMUEL FRANCIS SMITH, D.D.

TUNE—"*God Save the King.*"

My Country, 'tis of of thee,
Sweet land of liberty,
    Of thee I sing;
Land where my fathers died,
Land of the pilgrims' pride,
From every mountain side,
    Let freedom ring.

My native country,—thee,
Land of the noble free,
    Thy name I love;
I love thy rocks and rills,
Thy woods and templed hills;
My heart with rapture thrills,
    Like that above.

Let music swell the breeze,
And ring from all the trees
      Sweet freedom's song;
Let mortal tongues awake,
Let all that breathe partake,
Let rocks their silence break—
      The sound prolong.

Our father's God—to Thee,
Author of liberty,
      To Thee we sing;
Long may our land be bright,
With freedom's holy light;
Protected by Thy might,
      Great God, our King.

OUR FLAG—PAST, NOW AND FOREVER.

CELIA WHIPPLE WALLACE.

In childhood's sunny hours, with rare and sweet
      delight,
   Our country's Flag I **saw by** gallant hands un-
      furled,
And floating on the air—bright as a tropic bird—
   Beneath the June-blue sky, above our own home
      world.
The rocky wall of mountains 'round my village home
   Seemed a strong fortress, a God-set and sure defense.
A rhythmic moving band of stalwart martial men,
   Held in the circling arms of God's omnipotence,

Emblessed with power all wrong and evil to undo.
Beneath the waving flag of my loved native land,
With rapture swelled my childish and exultant form,
A bliss possessed me that I could not understand.

There fluttered in the graceful folds of that bright
flag
A mystic glory, like a shower of falling stars;
And, baptized in its rare, red rain of shining light,
I then and there became an armored child of Mars.

My perfect shield—the thrilling love of Fatherland—
That stayed the poisoned spears aimed at my in-
most heart—
Well was thou, then, the Fatherland of childhood
days;
But, now, my dear heart's only shelt'ring one thou
art.

My Country's Emblem, as thou wavest bright on
high,
A blessed charge thou hast—o'er Freedom's sons
to fly—
With stripes of Justice, and with stars of Love, unfurled,
Thou surely wilt, in time, enfranchise all the
world.

THE RETURN OF THE FLAGS OF THE VOLUNTEER REGIMENTS TO THEIR STATES.

BY ALFRED B. STREET.

Aye, bring back the banners and fold them in rest!
They have wrought their high mission, their holy
    behest!
Stained with blood, scorched with flame, hanging
    tattered and torn,
Yet dearer, by far, than when bright they were
    borne
        By brave hearts to glory!

As we gaze on their tatters, what battle fields rise,
Fields flashing in deeds of sublimest emprise!
When earth rocked with thunder, the sky glared
    with fire,
And Havoc's sad pinion dashed onward in ire!
        Deeds deathless in glory!

Press the Stars to the lips, clasp the Stripes to the
    heart!
Let us swear their grand memories shall never
    depart!
They have waved in this contest of freedom and
    right,
And our eagle shall waft them, wide streaming in
    light,
        To our summit of glory!

There—hope darting beacons, starred shrines, shall
    they glow,
Lighting liberty's way to the breast of the foe ;
Till her spear smites with splendor the gloom; and
    our sun,
One broad central orb, shall again brighten one
        Mighty nation of glory !

OUR FLAG.

GENERAL JOHN A. DIX.

" Across the wide-spread continent
    Our father's flag we bear ;
Each hill and dale, from shore to shore,
    The sacred sign shall wear,
And unseen hands shall strengthen ours,
    To hold it high in air,
      As we go marching on."

The ladies of New York, in sending a most elegant flag to their relatives and friends in the Seventh
Regiment, dedicated as follows :

"The flag of our country, what higher assurance
  Of sympathy, honor and trust could we send ?
The crown of our fathers' unflinching endurance,
  'Tis emblem of all you have sworn to defend :
Of freedom and progress, with order combined,
The cause of the Nation, of God and mankind."

If any one attempts to haul down the American
Flag, shoot him on the spot.—JOHN A. DIX.

BATTLE HYMN OF THE REPUBLIC.

JULIA WARD HOWE.

Mine eyes have seen the glory of the coming of the
    Lord,
He is trampling through the vineyard where the
    grapes of wrath are stored,
He hath loosed the fateful lightning of his terrible
    swift sword;
        His truth is marching on.

I have seen Him in the watchfires of an hundred
    circling camps;
They have builded Him an altar in the evening dews
    and damps;
I can read His righteous sentence by the dim and
    flaring lamps—
        His day is marching on.

I have read a fiery Gospel, writ in burnished rows of
    steel,
" As you deal with my contemners, with you my
    grace shall deal,
Let the hero, born of woman, crush the serpent with
    his heel,
        Since God is marching on."

He has sounded forth the trumpet that shall never
    call retreat,
He is sifting out the hearts of men before his judg-
    ment seat;

Oh! be swift, my soul, to answer Him! be jubilant,
    my feet!
        Our God is marching on!

In the beauty of the lilies Christ was born across the
    sea,
With a glory in his bosom that transfigures you and
    me;
As he died to make men holy, let us die to make
    men free,
        While God is marching on!

THE RED, WHITE AND BLUE.

BY EDWARD J. PRESTON.

O, glorious flag! red, white and blue,
Bright emblem of the pure and the true;
O, glorious group of Clustering stars!
Ye lines of light, ye crimson bars,
Always your flowing folds we greet,
Triumphant over all defeat;
Henceforth in every clime to be
Unfading scarf of liberty,
The ensign of the brave and free.

THE BOOK OF TIME.

" Out of monuments, names, words, proverbs, private records and evidences, fragments of stories, pas-
sages in books, and the like, we save and recover
somewhat from the deluge of time."—BACON.

www.ingramcontent.com/pod-product-compliance
Lightning Source LLC
LaVergne TN
LVHW090606210425
809137LV00009BA/623